# HAPPINESS WITHIN

## A JOURNEY OF REFLECTION AND SELF DISCOVERY

BY

TULSHI VARSANI

Copyright © 2023
Tulshi Varsani
All rights reserved

ISBN 9798854166416

Front cover image: Canva
Copyeditor: Sian Smith Editorial

Tulshi is a highly experienced coach with a passion for supporting both corporate and extreme sports clients to enhance their wellbeing and performance.

She applies research led practices to monitor and test, enabling her clientele to achieve long-term growth and development.

Tulshi was the first performance manager and coach for the 8x World Championship winning Formula One Team.

This book is dedicated to my parents.

To my wonderful mum and dad: thank you for supporting me and my brother. For always giving us room to flourish within anything we were interested in and passionate about. I am grateful to have such a close bond with you both.

Thank you for being my wonderful angels on Earth and always giving me and my brother everything we needed.

Thank you for your hard work, your sacrifices, and efforts. To this day you always have and always continue to give us more than enough.

Love always,
Your baby girl.

# CONTENTS

Introduction .................................................................................... 1

Chapter One: Authentically You ............................................. 9

Chapter Two: Happiness Looks Like ................................... 25

Chapter Three: Woes of Worrying ....................................... 41

Chapter Four: What is Happiness? ...................................... 59

Chapter Five: To Be Optimistic or Not to Be Optimistic: Is It Even a Question? ................................................................. 73

Chapter Six: Share your smile .............................................. 89

Chapter Seven: My Love Affair ........................................... 101

Chapter Eight: Conscious Eating ........................................ 119

Chapter Nine: You Snooze, You Win ................................. 133

Chapter Ten: I Am Grateful For You ................................... 149

Chapter Eleven: The Storm Will Pass ................................ 163

Chapter Twelve: Thank You, Next ...................................... 179

Chapter Thirteen: Thrive with Intention .............................. 187

Chapter Fourteen: Zen as Fu*k .......................................... 201

Chapter Fifteen: Positive Evaluation .................................. 217

Chapter Sixteen: Begin with One Step ............................... 225

References ......................................................................... 230

Acknowledgements ............................................................ 246

# INTRODUCTION

Everyone has their own story. Like many before me, the inspiration behind mine was when I realised how much life is a journey. This journey is something many people go through: self-discovery, transformation, self-realisation, and becoming. I've captured the details of some of my life's trials and tribulations within these chapters.

I've craved logging information ever since the age of eleven. It was around that time my brother and I were given our very first computer. We knew it was expensive to buy a computer back in the day. My dad (a labourer within the construction industry) did everything he could so we'd feel privileged. Instead of hiring external contractors he would learn new skills and trades to save him money. I never knew how physically demanding these roles were as a child. Fortunately, my uncle (Dad's business partner) was strict with their work/life balance and refuted Dad's suggestion to work every day in the week. They compromised and allowed themselves one day off each week. To this day, I am thankful for this decision: the memories of my childhood are filled with family gatherings, picnics in the park, weekends at the beach. They shape my version of what happiness is: even to this day those memories bring me joy when I think back to my childhood.

My mum, whose ambitions were to become a nurse, was not given a chance to further her education after high school and she struggled to find a job. This frustrating period lasted for nine months until she finally landed a role in an accountancy firm which she absolutely loved. She adored her co-workers and the autonomy the role offered her. However, once she and my father married, everything changed for her. It is not unusual for Indians to have extended family members living under one roof. As a new wife, she was expected to serve all members in that house. She had no control over the way the household was run and the new head of the household, her mother-in-law, was the one who made the rules. Mum's responsibilities extended beyond contributing to the household income. My mother was required to take care of the family home and everyone residing in it. She was accountable for cooking every family meal, including providing lunches for the men of the house before they went to work each day. Her duties included: cleaning the house from top to bottom before leaving for her job; washing clothes and wiping the floors by hand, as well as tidying the kitchen. I can't help but think she was in a real-life Cinderella story, a labour that continued long after my brother and I were born.

When I was very young, I never considered myself to be from a working-class family (until I understood what that word meant) because my parents gave my brother and I everything we could possibly need growing up. I did not know back then how fortunate we were to have a television or a digital box. We moved house so that my brother and I lived closer to a better school. My dad was a huge advocate of education, saying on many occasions, 'I wished I'd studied more to get ahead in life.' That was how I knew we were working-class: the struggles he faced to give us everything we needed was a huge privilege. My parents always did the best they could, which included giving us a personal computer – a truly momentous occasion. At the time I thought this must be one of the most expensive things in our house, because it was placed in my parents' room.

Isn't it funny the things we remember so distinctly when we recall memories from our childhood? Our brain is wired to make memories by using several different parts of the brain. The brain is clever in making associations from incoming information. This is the same when we listen to our favourite song: nostalgia takes us back to the very moment in time when we formed the memory listening to that song, drawing us back to the emotions we may have felt, and we can often remember what it was we were doing at the time. When we had our computer, one of the things I will never forget is the sound of dial-up internet. It was within this space that I started writing my own fictional novel. I thoroughly enjoyed reading fictional books as a child and I continued to crave this other world where I could be anyone else. A world where I could make up stories and imagine myself living in this alternative universe.

As I sit here, attempting to put my thoughts on paper for the introduction, I knew I had never lost my desire to write. However, because I have always seen myself as a below average student, I was unsure if this is something I could do; that it would simply remain a hidden dream. This aspiration to write sat in my heart for a long time, until the inspiration to write struck. A close friend and I were discussing our personal stressors over a coffee on a late summer's day in Brackley, when she suddenly queried how I had managed to process things that were difficult within my life. 'How can I bottle up what you have and take it with me?' she asked.

At the time, I was astounded that people would want to know why I am the way I am. But then I started to recall how they would ask how I dealt with situations, tackled negativity, faced challenges, and remained optimistic and positive in my outlook. That was the moment where I experienced the avalanche of questions. Questions upon reflection included, *What do you mean, there is something special about me?* I sat there, admiring my incredibly talented and smart friend. She was an engineer, someone who had discovered her passion for this field of work early on. She was upbeat, engaging, funny, and loved her job. She was also engaged to be married to her true love. Most importantly, to me she personified what wellbeing, success, and happiness were, and she radiated all of them from the inside out. This is where my thoughts gathered further momentum.

*What is the ultimate goal in life?*
*Is it to be happy?*

John Lennon's famous quote summarises how happiness can be set as its own intention in life:

*When I went to school, they asked me what I wanted to be when I grew up. I wrote down 'happy'. They told me I didn't understand the assignment, and I told them they didn't understand life.*
John Lennon

When looking at my own sense of happiness, I naturally wondered about what happiness looked like for other people in my life. My upbringing made it tricky to separate happiness from job satisfaction. When jobs are scarce there is less onus on personal satisfaction. When we have an abundance of jobs around us, our personal satisfaction counts for far more than its monetary value.[1] When we are self-reflecting within our working roles, we question ourselves regarding our overall levels of satisfaction. We seek gratification in the work we do, therefore the requirement to seek satisfaction overtakes the material reward. This outstrips the principal reason for working. When we can cover our basic needs, we seek to venture beyond our safety net and take our pursuit towards happiness more extremely.

Can differentiating between our job roles and overall satisfaction in life lead to answer the following question:

*What is it that makes us happy in our lives?*

The hours we spend each day in a job accumulate and make up a significant part of our lives. Is the pursuit to sustain the levels of happiness you seek within a professional domain, or is it simply a way of going through the motions in order to provide for your family? These answers will differ in respect to where you are regarding your levels of satisfaction in life. My parents had different experiences in this. They knew they needed to provide for their family: one loved their job, the other found it to be a necessity for contributing to the household income. The significance lies within the answer to these key questions:

*What makes me happy?*
*What are the conditions that nurture this level of happiness for us to sustain and thrive?*

Is it that once everything is synchronised within our lives, we are able to label it as happiness, fulfilment, and/or success? What drives our success to make us who we are today?

These questions allowed me to write thoughts about how we need to approach and reflect within our own lives. We can assess what our own needs and desires are and take control, without life leading us astray. Once I spoke to my friend over coffee, it instinctively occurred to me that I could reflect upon my personal journey and the result is this book. I have kept a journal as a means of reflection throughout my adult life, particularly as a practitioner coaching strength and conditioning. I discovered writing is an opportunity to assess and contemplate events. Reflecting and journaling became a tool to navigate through my problems and create solutions. Writing also happened to be a key influencer in helping me through personal struggles. This book was written while I was still recovering from significant setbacks in my life, some of which occurred while I was still actively working on my mindset. The combination of research and writing allowed me to build a breadth of knowledge into understanding my own emotional pathway and consequently (directly or otherwise) I knew I was able to nurture the ability to be more sympathetic towards others and heighten my emotional intelligence.

Everyone's journey is different. We all experience different levels of distress, discomfort, anguish, and heartache but this book was created to shine some light on some of my personal encounters. My childhood was an extremely happy one. My brother and I were brought up in a loving, kind, protected home, and I was able to pursue various dreams through the support of my family. This book allowed me to be vulnerable and write down some of my experiences that have made me who I am today. This book was written to showcase some of my vulnerabilities, in hope that you may also uncover some of yours. My hope is that through this journey you can discover your best self and create habits of success and happiness along the way.

This is a personal journey of self-discovery and within each chapter I will provide some hard-hitting questions that may support your own pursuit to discover your own happiness – in the 'Time to Consider' sections. These include practical tools and tips to expand your version of success and unleash your potential. On a practical note, I suggest you create a separate notepad or journal to write down your answers.

On a more personal note, some of my personal recollections make shock you, but I have aimed to provide a truly honest account of the various impactful events from my life in the hope that you, too, will not shy away from past events that you may feel like shying away from. You need to be able to look back at previous experiences with self-compassion and without judgement in order to answer the questions I ask throughout the book honestly. You may want to bookmark the points where the questions are posed in order to answer them again at a later date and see how your answers have changed. I also encourage you not to become disheartened if you are either disappointed by your current answers or feel you don't have any answer at all. The more practical solutions offered are there to help shift your mindset and serve to assist you with any struggles. The main purpose is to heighten your awareness surrounding any pervading problems or thoughts in your life and come up with an active solution. I now call any new problems an opportunity.

There may be some chapters you resonate with, others you may not. Some chapters centre on moments of realisation and personal recollection ('Authentically You', 'Conscious Eating', and 'The Storm Will Pass') while others offer more practical tips on changing your mindset ('Conscious Eating', 'My Love Affair' and 'You Snooze, You Win'). The chapters on intention setting and meditation come *after* detailing breakthrough periods in my life. Though these episodes in my life were traumatic and stressful, I was able to overcome them because of the work I did beyond the more practical aspects of sleep, exercise, and food (the standard triad any health practitioner would recommend). I would not advise trying to change too much at once: for me, once I had tackled the basics I found these other forms of self-development were a natural progression. Even though there is no set plan for everyone, taking these steps towards self-development will allow you to develop your own synergy, which will form a personal holistic approach, this will allow you to set your own blueprint in which you will incorporate wellness into your life.

Throughout this book I have woven in my own light-hearted but insightful stories, in a bid to support your own experiences. Whatever you are going through is totally fine and you will always have a choice to change things that happen to you.

I believe that often things are happening for you, and it is about empowering yourself to realise it will always be within your superpower to choose exactly what it is that is right for you.

You will see how I had to retrain myself to become positive. It was hard work initially, but this mindset has become more natural – I believe the same can happen to you. I am thankful and have enjoyed each moment of this journey: from putting my thoughts on paper to researching materials for supporting evidence, and even the hours of editing. Thank you for giving it a chance, for picking up this book and taking time to read this, taking time for you, and allowing me to express my inner thoughts and experiences.

*Life is a journey: not to see the world but to find yourself, your place in the world, and discover your own happiness. It is not a destination to be reached, but a journey to be enjoyed. Maybe your journey isn't so much about becoming anything, maybe it's unbecoming everything that isn't really you, so you can be who you were meant to be in the first place.*

Tulshi Varsani

## CHAPTER ONE: AUTHENTICALLY YOU

*Once you open the door to live a life where you are authentic to who you are and meant to be, you won't need to look back.*
Tulshi Varsani

*I've always been my worst critic* – does this sound familiar to you? Is being self-critical something you tell yourself or maybe it is a term you use often when describing who you are to your friends or colleagues? Perhaps you have purposefully explained why you are tough on yourself, demand more of yourself when it comes to work, family, or projects you undertake. There are times when some people want to showcase how hard they are on themselves. Some people acknowledge it as underlying bravado, perhaps to let people know something about them and their characteristic. For others, it is a gateway to openly criticising themselves. On occasion it can be used in the premise of being more thoughtful or self-aware, but often it seems like it is conditioned into us that to be successful we need to be highly critical of ourselves or own this formidable character trait. For some, this term may be considered an admirable quality, which they like to associate themselves with. Being self-critical is easy for many, particularly in people who tend to overthink.

I previously thought being self-critical showcased my work ethic and my need to constantly strive for better. However, I have come to understand that this was detrimental to my wellbeing. For me, being self-critical was working without boundaries and appeasing people sitting in the same negative bubble. I sought to be and do everything for everyone, only realising (almost too late) that it was not sustainable. I would be pulling myself apart to please others, reach above and beyond other people's expectations – and countless times there would be no acknowledgement regarding the effort I put in. Where was the return for being this self-critical in myself and my own work? This habit had become ingrained in me and it became a standard way of working. Constantly striving for more, never feeling good or worthy enough, left me feeling unappreciated and led to increasing self-criticism. It was only through the commitment to my spiritual practice that I became aware of the complete lack of boundaries placed for myself or others.

Self-criticism became a detriment to my health, and it was my responsibility to identify and omit critique from my daily life. I needed to flip this harsh inner critic on its head, to express more self-compassion to myself, in order to strengthen my positive traits whilst staying true to who I was.

*Look after yourself.*

This is not to say thinking one way and then thinking another came as easily as flipping a light switch. It was more like dismantling the socket rewiring; changing internal distribution and reassembling to get the best of the energy I was using. This type of work wasn't a quick fix either. Throughout my early adult life I'd experienced panic attacks and periods of depression during times when I never really understood the terminology. People who didn't know me thought I was fine and functioning well, but (thank goodness) my close friends saw me differently.

It was a few years ago, on a gorgeous summer's weekend in June. It was the day after a late night at a concert in London and my friends had stayed the night at my apartment. We were all tired, but I was feeling exceptionally exhausted. I presumed it was from lack of sleep from the night before, as well as recovering from a long working week. My friends observed me depleted on the sofa. They, too, were tired, but they noticed it was not in my nature to look or act this way. It was at that moment my friend said a shocking statement that raised the alarm bells in my head:

'If you continue this path, it will lead to self-destruction and you will eventually suffer a breakdown. I've been there and you are heading in that right direction unless you stop it now.'

A friend gave me this advice since she had experienced exhaustion herself. She spoke about her familiarity with burnout and that for her it had been too late to recognise. No one gave her the early warning to halt the breaks on her self-destruction and she struggled for months to recoup from the after-effects of her breakdown. The toll it took on her mental and physical health was completely overwhelming and all-consuming.

Two things came to mind as she spoke. The first was that I had no idea this had happened to her. The second was I remember thinking this was the first time I had heard her speak this way. Her tone was harsh with an undertone of desperation, that maybe her suffering would not have been in vain if she can warn and support someone else through her cruel life lesson. When she warned me in this manner, I was dumbfounded and at the time was unable to respond. I did not think my levels of exhaustion were a big deal; I excused it as being tired.

As they left for their drive back to Cardiff, I was reminded that under no circumstances was I to go outside. You need to understand that I am a moth to a flame when it comes to the outdoors and sunshine. There is something about the fresh air, the touch of sunlight on my skin that fills up my batteries, no matter how I am feeling. Nature is my key to rejuvenation; it is my re-energiser. As I looked outside, desperate to venture out fearing I would be missing out on the day if I did not, my friend's warning persisted: 'Open the French doors, let the air in, but take today to relax.' Despite feeling annoyed by being given instructions on what to do, mentally I gave in. Fighting against their request and battling with my body was one fight I simply did not have left in me and so I stayed indoors.

My friend's warning rang clear through my head for days after: that I needed to start taking care of myself. This disconnect between how I thought I was feeling and actually listening to my body was completely against who I was as a performance coach. For far too long, the media influenced people (and even athletes) to keep pushing, ignore the pain but slowly this narrative is changing. I had experienced anxiety and depression within various moments in my life, and my friend's warning made me aware that I was ignoring what my body was trying to tell me.

*Feeling the need to be busy all the time is a trauma response and fear-based distraction from what you'd be forced to acknowledge and feel if you slowed down.*
Unknown

Do you ever have a feeling when you are in a situation or meet someone, and your gut intuitively tells you something is not right? Why do we often dismiss this, especially when later we find we were right all along? If only we listened to our body and intuition from the beginning, it may have saved us a lot of time, energy, and potential heartache. I had unwittingly created a separation between trusting myself, my decisions, and my gut, and I had become withdrawn from my authentic connection. I'd gotten to the point where I felt I could no longer trust myself, particularly when it had led me to a series of bad relationships. I mistrusted my intuition and allowed my negative thoughts and anxious feelings to distract me from the true instinctive signs I was blatantly ignoring.

I realised those moments of heartache and pain did not happen in *absence* of good intuition, but because I had chosen not to listen to or trust it. My deluded mindset and disconnect meant I could not see the wood for the trees. I understood my immediate attention required me to refocus and be present. I was familiar with my soundtrack, which I played repeatedly like a popular song over the radio; I would recall memories from my past or race through thoughts about potential outcomes in the future. Once I set the intention to focus on the present moment, to gain clarity and peace within my thoughts, that was the beginning of my incredible journey ... but little did I know how long this would take.

*It's about the journey, never the destination.*
                                            Simon Rattle

Worry cannot add a single hour to our lives, research shows that focusing on the past can have mental health benefits, because you are condemned to repeat the past if you cannot remember it. A reason why people in the West are more focused on the present is because they are focused on themselves. Independence means they are not as concerned about how their present behaviour will affect past or future relationships. Consequently, extreme focus on self-narcissism can result in depression for oneself and for others[1,2,3,4].

As weeks rolled by, despite being less physically fatigued, I could feel an internal struggle envelope me; it caused me to feel tightness around my chest and I struggled to understand why there was this overwhelming feeling of unhappiness. I was in an industry I loved, I liked my job, yet something was amiss. I sensed this inner conflict but was unable to pin down where it originated from. Until a serendipitous moment struck a chord with me towards my soul's pathway.

It was another glorious summer day: rays of sunshine filtered through my apartment, lighting up the living room where I practised yoga and meditation, when suddenly something caught my attention. A video had popped up as a recommended watch list: it was from Gabrielle Bernstein's *The Universe Has Your Back*.[5] I had this old sensation return; it was a trigger from my gut, that intuitive feeling I had since become unfamiliar with. This trigger urged me to watch it, much like a gravitational pull circling my orbit. Since I made it an intention to nurture and listen to my intuition and gut reactions, I pressed play on the remote. And it was life-altering.

This is something I can only describe as an 'ah ha!' moment – a notion popularised by Oprah Winfrey on her talk show. This shook me into a moment of clarity and awakening: it was when the penny finally dropped. Gabrielle spoke about her work and personal evolution. Whilst I watched her story unfold, my immediate judgement was how she was so poised and beautiful. It was a false assumption that she seemed to have everything in her life under her control, but in her story she described her struggle in detail.

Gabrielle's words truly resonated with me: she was not perfect, and she didn't have everything under control. Her internal battle was our familiar battle. She placed her vulnerability out into the audience by describing ways she would control every aspect of her life, within a given timeline. As an individual who adores a plan, this battle became all too familiar to me. For me, as a young Indian girl, I was conditioned into thinking I needed to go to school, get a decent job, get married to a nice Indian man, have children – and that's life. (I am quite sure this is not unique to being Indian, but it was what I knew.) Surprisingly, as I was getting older, the pressure lessened around me and I separated myself from the Indian community a little more – or maybe it was because they thought I was far too old (for a woman in her early-thirties, you're over the hill). Despite the lack of enforcement from other Aunties,*the pressure remained within.

I had become so conditioned, becoming my own critic asking questions such as, *why aren't you married yet, what is wrong with you?* Instead of dealing with why I was asking myself these questions, I pushed aside the internal chatter by diverting my energy to focus on my work. Ignorance proved bliss because work was something I felt I could be in control of. I controlled my options, work hours, time, energy, and application on projects. I know now all this did was provide an unhealthy distraction. Instead of tackling my insecurities and lack from within, I delved into work because it would solidify my need to control outcomes by distracting myself from areas outside of my control. Work proved to be my attempt to control situations instead of confronting my internal resistance.

---

* 'Auntie' is the term for older Indian women even if they are of no relation.

Have you ever wanted something in life, but you questioned it before you had it? We all do this to some degree. Take the following as an example. You have suddenly become irritated and fed up with work: you see your friend post picture of a beautiful holiday destination and consider looking into taking a break for yourself. You go online and search for this destination and find it is quite expensive. Suddenly you become annoyed that you may not be able to afford it, until you notice an advert with an offer to another destination, equally as stunning, if not more. White sandy beaches, crystal blue water, and sunshine highlighting its beauty. You delve into your search and become obsessed with this new destination until you experience some internal hesitation, something you may not be aware of, a sense perhaps it is too good to be true. Nevertheless, you keep investigating and search for suitable dates. The dates on offer are not suitable for you. You decide you cannot possibly take that specific date off, sensing your boss would not grant it (despite having plenty of leave available). You convince yourself it would be a waste of money anyway; that it is better you do not blow your savings on some adventure when it is best to be more conservative. That money may come in handy in case of an emergency. You decide you will take a break over a weekend, somewhere local with a friend. That weekend never happened.

All this elaborate flirting with potential joy, excitement, and adventure peaked as quickly as it became diminished due to your internal conflict and reflective thinking which regurgitated old patterns and a familiar internal dialogue. This is not to say your hesitations are not valid – particularly when making a judgement call on your finances. This is just one example elucidating someone going through one version of internal struggle and self-sabotage. I know someone who did this in relationships. He would commit wholeheartedly to a relationship, move in with his partner, yet some years later, it ended. He self-sabotaged his relationships when things got too much for him. Of course, all relationships are different, but many people are unaware they carry burdens and insecurities into their new relationship, before dealing with problems from past relationships.

The result of my friend's intervention followed by recognising myself in Gabrielle Bernstein's words created an almost instant decision to live more in the present and critique myself less. My journey allowed me to tap into my newfound compassion and within it I understood my need to tackle a few difficult questions.

1) **How can I treat myself well?**

2) **How can I be more compassionate and kinder to myself?**

3) **What does this entail?**

4) **What is the rationale behind self-sabotages?**

5) **In what way do I sabotage myself?**

6) **Is there a pattern of self-sabotage?**

7) **What am I hiding from?**

8) **What am I afraid of?**

9) **What do I want?**

All of these were and are heavily loaded questions: the important thing is to not feel pressure to come up with the answers right away.

Many of those answers came to me during quiet moments of reflection or through meditation. Often, I would find answers whilst journaling. The answers evolved from weeks and months of focused attention and practice using various tools. I began to understand we exert control over things we think we need to and can handle. Humans like being in control: it feels reassuring and we develop a sense of comfort and safety within this realm.

I was all too familiar with my *relationship bias*, because secretly I carried with me the need to keep people at bay. I felt fear that if anyone would become too close I would end up being hurt. I would use countless excuses and became incredibly successful in pushing people away (including friends and potential partners) because this fear stemmed from within – and I perpetuated those results. That self-sabotage wasn't because of an absence of fruitful relationships, in fact I had a wonderful example of what a loving and loyal relationship looked like because I grew up seeing my parents who provided me with the example of what a loving, loyal, and committed relationship looked like. I encountered first-hand the ways they were affectionate with one another (even if as a teen it was not always appreciated). Despite that, I developed personal hang-ups about feelings of being unworthy, about not being good enough, and eventually convinced myself that I didn't need it.

Allowing fear, neglect, and potential heartache prevented me from forming loving, meaningful relationships, it was another form of control and self-harm. I would control my work, my education, and the achievements in my career to divert the potential to be happy in discovering fulfilling relationships. This way I could manage the risk versus reward and the outcome meant I couldn't get hurt by someone else. I wouldn't tell anyone how I felt. I was ashamed that I couldn't sustain a relationship. I would not allow myself to be judged or shamed by other people and give them the opportunity to ask the question I frequently asked myself, *what's wrong with you?*

Thinking like this was when I fell into my personal black hole. Within it lay my insecurities such as not being worthy enough, beautiful enough, funny enough, or not being 'enough' for love. It took a lot of focused internal analysis and listening to my truth to uncover those fears. I discovered it stemmed from a younger version of myself growing up with this internal fear. The fear of abandonment and being unlovable. As an adult, I made this my reality.

Another penny dropped when Gabrielle spoke about listening to herself and her intuition, to lessen the grip on control and focus on what is thriving instead. As a result, I refocused my attention and used my energy and effort on what was thriving instead of what was missing. For me, this meant opening my eyes towards the people and love I was surrounded by. This entailed changing my perspective, particularly regarding the people within it. I needed to come to terms with my past (which I did by letting it go) and release the hold and control regarding possible outcomes in my future. I finally accepted a lot was beyond my control and that isn't a bad thing. This reinforced the need to be present and grateful within the moment.

*God dreams bigger things for you, than you ever could.*
*Unknown*

Taking time to uncover the answers to the questions above took persistent effort. I needed to come to terms with my past and the situations I had been through before I could step into the type of person I wanted to be. I needed to let go of self-destructive habits (abusing food and exercise) as well as release the need to be in full control. Instead, I sought to lower the barriers I had placed before my friends and when forming new relationships. I started to deal with other traumas from my childhood. I began to understand the calculated risks to increase my levels of happiness and I began to accept my worth. The compassion I nurtured opened a pathway to being kinder, more loving, and more considerate to myself – and in turn to others around me. I sought to be a better version of myself, benefiting my own wellbeing and that of others. Letting go of self-criticism from the past allowed me to come to terms with the woman I am today and see how everything I'd been through was purposeful.

I began to nurture my intuition, to release the control I thought I needed to have on my future and allow myself to surrender to what is meant for me. I began to trust myself more and over time I realised the love I craved so badly needed to grow from within. To cultivate and flourish love, appreciation and acceptance, and remove self-criticism allowed me to appreciate all the things which encompassed the love that was already thriving in my present existence. What I did not know is how valuable treating myself meant. With that insight things begin to flow into moments that made life more beautiful. My awareness shifted and I could see love flourish everywhere because my attention and attitude altered.

Having confidence, compassion, empathy, and showing kindness to yourself will allow you to be more of those things for others. You will extend more compassion and empathy towards those around you, simply because you know you have it within you and you will extend it into the world. When we are kinder to ourselves it allows us to be kinder to others. Have you ever been told bullies are bullying because they are dealing with something themselves, that maybe they are jealous of you in some way, or maybe they are hurting so they want to hurt you? Think back to a time when you recognised someone was in a bad mood and, as a consequence, they may have shown anger towards you. Their anger is their own struggle, inner conflict, or hardship. If we know the individual we find we can excuse their behaviour, but if we do not know them well we can end up reflecting their current mood.

    A bad mood or an angry comment can spread like a forest fire, particularly if it triggers something in you. Deflecting anger or a bad mood onto another person such as a colleague, a friend, or even towards your partner is fairly common and we end up resenting the person for sharing their vexation. Conversely, experiencing a smile from a stranger, enjoying a compliment, or sharing a joke with someone connects us. It draws us closer and allows us to be vulnerable and happier: this is also a gift we can afford to share. When we are loving to ourselves, when we release any trauma or burdens, when we respect and value ourselves, we give the best version of ourselves to ourselves and then to others.

Self-love took time. It took me at least 18 months to acknowledge what this feels like (in addition to 20 plus years prior to this realisation). Giving yourself love, compassion, consideration, and letting go of the inner critic – particularly when things aren't going the way you envision – means you can ease off the internal pressure you may be fighting within. You can also reduce the need to control the circumstance and its outcome. When we turn down the dial and reduce the pressure of trying to control the outcome, we quieten our self-criticism and tap into the frequency of our intuition for signs or opportunities for more love and happiness to filter into our existence.

These days, my intuition leads me to make the right decisions for the outcome I desire. At first it was extremely hard to quieten the noise, the mindless chatter, and internal dialogue, as it often involved self-depreciation, but this is crucial when attempting to tap into your intuitive frequency. I realised that once I used meditation to quieten my thoughts I exerted more self-compassion on myself, even during difficult practices. I also noticed more and more 'coincidences' occurring in my life. Every time I asked for something, I would receive it. Over time, I learnt that employing a nonattachment to the outcome was empowering. Whether you believe in God, are religious or not, whether or not you believe in a higher power or are spiritual, nothing is random or happens by chance.

There are many kinds of probability: subjective probabilities, evidential probabilities, and objective chances, to name a few. We often describe something as random if it happens by chance. Scientists use chance, or randomness, to mean that when physical causes can result in any of several outcomes, we cannot predict what the outcome will be in any particular case.[6] Some philosophers are equally subjected to this elision, but others connect chance and randomness deliberately. It is also intuitively plausible that if an event is truly random it cannot be explained. However, if it happens for a reason, it isn't truly random.[7]

The concept of order maintained by the law of cause and effect is a scientific principle traceable through Hebrew, Babylonian Greek, and modern civilisation. The law of cause and effect explains that every thought of intention, action, and emotion transmitting from you, as a person, sets into motion an unseen chain of effects, which vibrates into the entire cellular structure within the environment, thus into the cosmos. Eventually, the vibrational energy returns to the original source upon the swing of the pendulum. With the knowledge of this and evidence from coincidences, this underpinned my sense of power in something bigger than myself. I began to understand there was a greater universal truth and within that I was able to tap into this higher realm and alternate dimensions.

This, of course, gave me a greater sense of empowerment, particularly in moments when I felt lost or unable to see the bigger picture from turbulence I faced personally or at work. I began to think outside my small existence and felt that there was more happening that I wasn't aware of. I can only describe this as feeling assured; that I drew comfort in knowing there was something bigger at play, but something I can contribute towards writing my own destiny. It gave me a sense of self-assurance and enabled me to delve deeper, seek confidence within my intuition and navigate towards being true to what my purpose was within this life. This was a lightbulb moment, which I still value to this day. It meant I could loosen my grip on controlling the way I wanted my life to go by accepting what it is I am here to do alongside the realisation that during that journey, things will arise that are purposefully connected to that goal. I borrowed this from Gabrielle's talk: when she asked for guidance, she sought to let go of her control and allow for the things that were supposed to be, be.

Even to this day I use this prayer, I speak it into the cosmos when I ask for guidance to align me to my true purpose in life.

*Dear Universe,*
*What would you have me do?*
*Where would you have me go?*
*What would you have me say and to whom?*
Gabrielle Bernstein.[5]

This small yet powerful prayer (or call it guidance, if you prefer) served my higher purpose into understanding why I am here on Earth. It allowed me to relinquish the control I so desperately held onto. It enabled me to let go of the tight grip in wanting or needing to control every aspect of my life. It facilitated me to give up the attachment to the outcome and goal of where I *think* I need to be and gave me the freedom in faith towards the unknown. It has also given me faith in asking for my purpose, whilst I am a spiritual being experiencing human existence on this Earth. It has given me faith on days when I need additional support and guidance towards making the right choices, or simply to stop forcing an outcome and allow greater opportunities to flow to me. And they did!

There were often times when I would ask for help and announce this prayer to the world and the universe at large, when I openly allowed and accepted the lessons it brought me that day. This prayer always gave me the level of certainty I needed because I was able to let go of the need to feel in control. I was able to place the control outside myself without the burden I placed within myself. It gave me confidence, knowing that whatever situation arose, including hardships, I accepted the lesson and trusted it would pass, and I would no longer linger on *why* it happened or ruminate over what was. On those days when I recited it, I found it led me to opportunities and circumstances that accelerated my journey into self-realisation. It also allowed me to be grateful for the day and all the new lessons that came within it.

Mere coincidences were not just coincidences anymore and thoughts of seeking out support and then speaking to people who could help me on my personal and professional journey, all came about at the right time. When I succumbed to that particular moment in time, when I allowed the moment to play out as it was, I was in a state of allowance. It was then I received the guidance I needed. I began to use this feeling of release and remained open to opportunities, which also led me to increase my intuition. When something didn't feel right and I didn't know what to do, I'd ask for guidance and allow the answers to arrive, instead of pushing towards (what can be) an unfavourable outcome through sheer force. When that happened, it allowed me to understand what I needed to work through. It was showing me the internal resistance I held onto and how much I was replaying my old habits of self-sabotage, where I sought to control the outcome. It was in that negative, desperate state when things I desired would often be pushed further away. Throughout this journey I realised the need to be patient, release the rigid expectations of a specific outcome desired, and be open to new opportunities, adventures, and circumstances. If I let go of the control, I wouldn't be disappointed but instead would be open to the probability of something better coming along. I was increasing the sense of probability that nothing was random, everything was for a reason, even if I didn't know what that reason was at the time. As a result of releasing expectations and control, the things I once wrote in my journal or described on my vision board started to become a reality.

## TIME TO CONSIDER

1) **What are you afraid of?**
   This answer can only come from a place of truth. You must be completely honest with yourself for this to be a breakthrough moment. Don't be afraid to ask yourself this question numerous times.
   
   Eliminate the need to change: simply observe your patterns, habits, and things you have been through and why you are afraid.
   
   The key is to change nothing, but simply accept what you are feeling.

2) **What are you attempting to control?**
   We may want to form a tight grip over the things we want, but this often leads to higher expectations when they do not work out as we wanted and therefore lead us to feel disappointment.
   - Instead of placing the happiness on the outcome, place awareness on what it is you are attempting to control and why.

- Why do you have this need to control the situation and what are your expectations of them?
- Did these expectations stem from things you are afraid of?

Remember to be compassionate with yourself; practise self-love and patience. Many things may arise in the present that you had not previously considered.

3) **Where did those feelings stem from?**

4) **What other feelings do you associate with this?**

5) **What is it you can do, right now, to change the circumstance? Or are you able to accept them for what they are?**

Unless you can change the circumstance, it may prove beneficial to divert your attention away from it. If this is something you want or have desired, give it some time. Sit with the feelings, allow inspiration to strike you to make a move and if it does not feel right, learn to trust your instincts. Let it go and wait to see what happens next. Letting go does not mean giving up, it means you are releasing it from your attention and doing other things whilst you wait for what is truly meant for you to arrive.

Having patience for things to unfold can be scary but learning to sit back and not interfere is also a great tool to use when pursuing something great.

## CHAPTER TWO: HAPPINESS LOOKS LIKE

I remember my stomach churning; I was not sure what to expect. I was dressed as if heading to a business meeting: heels, aubergine coloured pencil skirt, black blazer. This was my power play move: dressing well enabled me to fake the confidence I needed. Parking up my car, I stepped out and felt a little like Elle Woods in *Legally Blonde* as I walked towards the reception. As the doors slid open, I introduced myself and it wasn't until I sat down that it suddenly dawned on me.

I was finally here. My dreams were coming true. I was two weeks away from starting my role within a three-time World Championship Formula One team and I was here for an intro tour. It felt as if I was in a bubble, like I was gliding into another big challenge of my life, and I remember thinking to myself, *is this what happiness and success feels like*?

This seemingly perfect time in my life was almost exactly a year before I would vow to change my mindset and approach to my wellbeing and outlook on happiness and success. After starting my dream job, the first few months flew by in what seemed like a smoky haze. Without realising, I was slowly sinking deeper into a new struggle within my life. The struggle was between balancing working all the hours I could to get ahead and taking care of my personal wellbeing. During those first few months, I most certainly neglected my personal and social wellbeing as I blurred the lines between passion and obsession. Sometimes when a person reaches a peak within their life, accomplishing a long-term goal – as I had striving to get into Formula One (F1) – they may think and believe they can finally relax because they've finally made it.

Made it to the destination they'd dreamed of being in as a child. What real life teaches you is that there is no final destination: there is simply a destination, before it all becomes new again. This was another new beginning: a new adventure and another fresh start. When we win at a game of monopoly, that is it. We start a new game; we start from scratch and each time we start from the bottom. That is how it felt when I reached that position in F1.

Getting the job was where all my effort had been directed; now new challenges developed within each phase that followed. When do we reach a point where we feel we have 'made it', reached the success we fought and worked so hard for? Is there a moment we can identify as being successfully happy?

I was in F1 and although this brought me joy and happiness because I'd reached a point in my career where I was in the industry I loved; in my heart this was not the pinnacle of my success. What I knew for sure was I needed to work harder to find what my next dream was. Getting the role in F1 gave me a huge step in the right direction but there was something else, something more I needed to pursue. In this phase of my career I created a new space which I later discovered would be my home away from home.

I had always neglected to be in the present moment and enjoy accomplishments achieved because I quickly refocused my attention and energy onto my next goal. These goals were always written within my five to ten-year plan. Having reached a goal to be within F1, I decided to take a different direction, adopt a new strategy, and chose *not* to create a new 5-year plan. Instead, I choose to take the time to transition and focus on the here and now. My aim was to be present in the moments, be happy and enjoy what was happening around me. I wanted to take it all in and live in the moment. Those moments, however, passed quickly. A series of changes, beyond my control, forced me to figure out my next move, instead of living in the present moment as I had vowed to do.

Have you ever been in a position where you outgrew something or someone, and you realised you were no longer learning from the situation? Your ambition or passion has faded or that you simply needed another challenge? Sooner than I had expected, I was forced to move forward and pursue a vision for something bigger. Although it was a necessity, I knew it would not be easy. I'd tied myself around relationships I'd created, I valued the new connections I'd forged, and had freely anchored myself into an environment that allowed me to uncover a new sense of happiness. I'd also found happiness uncovering my personal wellbeing journey. I'd come to a point where I'd realised happiness included the acquaintances and friends I could rely on; I'd unearthed pleasure through breaking down my own barriers and being vulnerable. These discoveries made the decision to move on that much harder.

The consistency, income, and routine gave me the security I enjoyed: all things we are often told to aspire for in life. Yet beneath this security, I was becoming increasingly unhappy with changes happening around me. Stifling my creativity, undermining my work, stalling ways in which I could develop as a strength and conditioning coach. These unexpected changes forced me to rethink the direction I could take. Although we are taught that change is good for us, we tend to resist change because we are hindered by fear or because we are challenged within the area called 'the unknown'.

Along this journey I discovered I would often question the consistency within my state of happiness. What I uncovered and how I dealt with it will be explained within later chapters, but a meaningful lesson was understanding that throughout my journey, happiness comes and goes, just like the tidal waves from the ocean. Like all thoughts and emotions we experience throughout our day, they come and go as they please. Despite having created moments that made me feel joyful and fulfilled, and though I experienced moments of pure, genuine happiness, I tended to place happiness on things I had accumulated. By this I don't just mean material goods, but elements such as wonderful friends, building myself a home, finding success in my role as a manager and coach. But now this was all to change where would all my happiness go? Thankfully, at the point where the whole situation was completely taken out of my hands, I'd developed the tools to allow me to move forward. It was the security in knowing I'd created habits that would enable me to feel pure joy and happiness within those moments, that more moments would come throughout events in my life. These crucial habits are discussed in great detail in the middle chapters of this book, but it's important for you to understand we often can't test the efficacy of these habits until we face unexpected and difficult challenges.

You may be aware of the proverb 'time flies when you are having fun'. Have you ever watched a child playing? If you have not, take a moment to observe a child the next time you are able to watch them play with their favourite toy. Look at their facial expressions, their demeanour, how they are completely absorbed in their own world of imagination. You can see the pure enthusiasm within their facial expressions and concentration: for that moment in time they are focused and nothing else matters. Children are not thinking about anything other than being present, they are fully immersed in their imaginative play. When I gave myself time to stop and think about it, this was a similar feeling I'd encountered when I'd be immersed in the moment, even if I wasn't doing anything of significance. I imagined it would be the same expression of peace, joy, and happiness within each child playing with their toys.

After my friends forced me to re-evaluate my approach to work and life (and thank goodness they did) there were moments, particularly at the very beginning of my quest for happiness, I would recall feeling guilty about being happy (though at that point in my life, those moments felt rare). Instead of being in the moment, I would quickly derail this new train of thought, navigating myself away from that happy moment. Thoughts would creep in and contradict the state of happiness within myself. Suddenly the negativity of all the things I was unhappy about would surge through my thoughts like storm clouds brewing overhead and I couldn't stop it fast enough. These thoughts would cast grey shadows on my beaming rays of light I'd tried to generate in order to shift the focus on current conditions and challenges at work. Any moment of happiness was drowning in the storm clouds and all my thoughts were taking me from the present moment into another; reliving the past or worrying about my future.

Despite having solitary moments of happiness, my periods of self-reflection drew me back into a state of negativity. I would migrate from being in my happy bubble and move into a small, dark room which housed shadows of both my past and unpredictable future. In that room there was a different part of my character, someone who was extremely stern. She wrote questions on the walls such as *Why are you so happy? Is this where you really want to be in life?* and *You don't deserve this.* Sentences that would strip away any pleasures in life I'd experienced merely moments before. Within that room housed the pressure that I needed to prove myself and I must earn my success and happiness. I had somehow convinced myself those two nouns were in a relationship and were united, leaving me under the impression that there could not be one without the other.

Over time, I understood that momentary feelings of happiness are rare but can be created with consistency. The most important lesson about happiness was that it is always in the present. That it doesn't exist when thoughts are navigated into my past or future. When I started to practise being in the moment, my emotions were taken out of the equation and it was *my* responsibility to not put any emphasis on new thoughts. My agenda was to allow those thoughts to flow freely, just like waves in the ocean. What I eventually learnt was that it is perfectly fine to be happy in the moment *and* still have ambitions and goals to better your life.

Happiness is a personal and comparative emotion. We tend to measure our levels of happiness by using our experiences and degrees of sadness from our past as a measure to dictate our overall and current state. If you have ever encountered deeper levels of sadness then there is a chance you will have a higher degree of happiness.[1] There are, of course, some people who do not experience such highs or lows in terms of their levels of happiness. Herein lays the middle ground.

Protecting yourself against emotional pain (such as sadness) simultaneously restricts happiness. I always leant into this method to reduce my levels of sadness and limit the depth of personal relationships, but consequently this also limited my levels of happiness. Have you ever knowingly put people in a box and prevented them from being too close to you on a personal level? I made this decision to prevent myself from getting hurt: if I could control the level of connection with others, I could prevent myself against any emotional pain. As a result, I would prevent many people from entering my personal and emotional space and I successfully prevented myself from being hurt by pushing others away or keeping them at a distance. For some, this middle ground can enable relationships to develop quite normally, but when the levels of intimacy become too threatening, those relationships will either fade or die. This middle ground is like a black hole: it prevents any relationship from flourishing and progressing into a deeper connection. It is common to either intentionally or unintentionally sabotage personal relationships by preventing them from becoming too intimate. The people who are in this middle ground often see themselves as victims and ironically seek comfort in the people they hold at bay.[2]

We build walls to protect ourselves from emotional pain. The higher the walls, the greater the degree of emotional pain that has been experienced in the past. Only those who fear getting hurt again will build up higher walls – and they are built for one sole purpose; to keep people out. These walls are purposefully used to defend our personal and emotional space. These barriers can be used to disconnect from a part of the world where we may feel threatened. This disengagement includes happiness.[1] It includes keeping people (who may be able to show us happiness) at bay. By preventing this level of intimacy, we are blocking ourselves off from a part of our lives and choosing to remain victims for the rest of our natural life.

I'd decided that living in the fear of the unknown enhanced the fear of intimacy and therefore would limit any potential sadness or heartbreak. However, the best way we can bond and build relationships – thereby experiencing true intimacy –

is to share personal and/or common experiences. Perversely, couples form closer bonds when they struggle and survive trying times.[2]

In circumstances of stress (including natural disasters and terrorism) people reduce their personal boundaries and accept class divisions. Particularly around the time of 9/11, New York City residents who greeted one another on the street were more considerate and sensitive to one another; they were gentler than normal.[2] Stress prepares the body for resistance, it may also be the opportunity to experience beautiful things in life, such as connection, love, and happiness. Without struggle or some element of stress, happiness could not be measured. Pain is a part of life; we can try and prevent pain from occurring by protecting ourselves by creating barriers and boundaries based on our decisions on what we do and do not accept from others. If we feed our fears created from our previous experiences, we may continue to live in a state of worry. This worry contributes to the barriers we have built to protect ourselves against similar events repeating in the future and these are conscious choices. We can either increase our suffering from creating barriers and building walls, or we can deal with the pain. By dealing with the traumas and facing the sadness, we attempt to remain open, so we may be able to experience the highs happiness has to offer. This is by far more satisfying than experiencing the middle ground where we hide behind the wall created to block ourselves off from potential hurt.

This is all easier said than done, however. We may be scared to try again. After touching a hot pan, we learn not to do it again. These types of traumas and unpleasant feelings are embedded into our psyche; we have learnt from past experiences and may have developed a fear of failing. We may get too stubborn to open the new door and conditioned ourselves into dreading deception. Yet each new connection you make and person you meet is different to your experiences. Having this level of awareness of the pervading effect of previous events brings light into some potentially rigid thoughts you have been adhering to. This awareness is essential before you are able to change your attitude towards it. Many people are likely unaware of their personal self-sabotages – within themselves and within their relationships – which may cause them to potentially withdraw from experiencing a fuller, happier life.

Before we can change anything, we must first acknowledge the existence of what needs changing. Identifying what we are afraid of means taking some time to be quiet and seek answers within ourselves; this can be accomplished through personal reflection. The objective is to listen and understand what you truly feel about a particular situation or circumstance. Clarity becomes easier when we are given space and silence. If you are compassionate to yourself and are non-judgemental, this time can be invaluable in seeking solace within yourself. For me, this space became a time to enter openly and honestly. It was within this space I could understand what I was afraid of; then I could recognise what it was I truly wanted.

When you start this method, ensure you are free from judgement. Seek to understand yourself as if you were sitting opposite your best friend who is going through personal struggle. This reflective practice may allow you to become aware of something you may not have realised was affecting you. Using moments of stillness, silence, or meditation will guide you to look inwards, assess what you may be feeling and delve deeper into your intuition. Personally, this pathway gave me a chance to understand the reasons why I was blocking people out and why I was truly afraid of connecting. When I was able to confront those feelings from my past experiences, I could take steps to overcome them.

Here are some questions I want you to answer, within a safe space.

1. **Are you able to sit alone with your thoughts (without judgement) and acknowledge what you are feeling right now?**

2. **What are you most afraid of?**

## 3. How can you lean into this pain and accept it for what it is?

*If you feel anxiety or depression, you are not in the present. You are either anxiously projecting the future or depressed and stuck in the past.
The only thing you have any control over is the present moment [...]*

Tobe Hanson

Being immersed within the present moment meant I could feel joy, security, peace, and contentment, no matter what I was doing. Initially, however, this feeling was scarce and negativity or overthinking often took away from my experiences. I'd face what I can only describe as emotional tsunamis. I'd get angry and extremely frustrated when things did not go to plan, or how I had expected them to. Eventually, I learnt how to calm those tsunamis into waves. Much of that was from awareness, inner reflections, and seeing these examples from those whom I kept within my inner circle.

When I realised I could experience happiness in such fleeting moments, I also understood it wavered depending upon the situation. This realisation allowed me to reflect and question; *How can these momentary bursts of happiness become more consistent? How could I be happy now, despite my surroundings?* My aim was to find out how I could elongate those joyous experiences. If I could feel good, for no reason in particular, how could this state be enhanced and occur more frequently? If we can understand that our feelings and thoughts come in and out of our mind much like waves within each moment of each day, how can we ease the intensity of those waves – particularly when the weather changes into a storm?

When there is chaos going on around you, it can be easy to become frustrated, angry, or upset; these are common emotions and feelings. My awareness developed by observing what my common reactions were and then exploring why I was feeling those emotions. I'd come to understand that the only thing we are in control of is our emotions and actions. Amongst the chaos we tend to think we have no control, when in fact it is still within us. We get to choose our attitude and we get to choose our actions. Having pressing issues that need to be dealt with immediately need not take away your inner happiness about yourself or life in general. Yet during turbulent times we succumb to a negative state of mind and it feeds on our insecurities, anxieties, and fears. How can you replace those thoughts and emotions during the eye of the storm? Remain calm, under control, and take relevant actions instead of reacting to events around you?

As women we've been told we can have it all, we can do anything, and have everything we've wanted. I don't believe this to be true. I do believe we can have it all, but not all at once. I believe each of us has to make sacrifices in order to get what we want.

When I wanted to succeed in my career, I'd willingly make sacrifices in my personal relationships. I chose to be less social and disconnect with friends and I would be terribly picky about with whom I'd spend my time. This enabled me to succeed in my business and career and build a foundation, but I know without those sacrifices, I would not be where I am today.

I know women who had to go back to work sooner than they would have preferred after the birth of their child. One of my dear friends was torn between being the sole provider for her family and staying at home with her two young boys. The sacrifice she made was time spent with her boys in order to provide them with what they needed: a stable home and a fruitful future.

I also know plenty of successful male coaches, engineers, and managers who have sacrificed time with their loved ones because of the sport they are in. It could be football, rugby, or F1: their working schedules were gruelling and all-consuming. It most certainly affected the relationships they had with their wives, partners, and children.

We may have a life filled with challenges and turmoil; we may also need to make sacrifices in order to experience delayed gratification, but it's up to us where we find our happiness. There is a clear distinction between happiness obtained from things and happiness we feel from within. Having things we want – either right now or in the future – takes certain levels of sacrifice. Some may believe accruing material items will make them happier, and for a short while this may be true. Some may feel happier chatting to a friend, eating an ice cream, or watching funny videos online; but these are still just momentary bursts of happiness. They exist and they are fleeting. Television, social media, shopping, and sex are all examples of immediate pleasures. It is said true happiness does not come from accomplishments or things, but that it is in the journey you have taken to get there. Therefore, if happiness is found in the journey, how can we find happiness in the mundane, the ordinary, and within each day? How can we cultivate awe in the everyday?

When you find joy and happiness in the simple pleasures stated above, they are short-lived. Gratification from superficial means, such as a compliment from a stranger or likes on social media, is reliant on an external source. This means that when individuals experience happiness highs that do not originate from within, there is likely to be an experience of parallel lows when faced with negative exchanges.

Place yourself in a situation where your friend told you their mum, sister, or friend does not like you; how would you feel?

How about if you posted something on your social media platform and received a ton of backlash; what happens to your state of happiness?

If you were trying to help someone at work and they came back blaming you for a bad outcome – perhaps even telling other people not to trust you – what emotions would arise within you?

If people cling to happiness brought by simple pleasures or external sources, there is a chance their experience of happiness is dependent upon a specific outcome. The issue most people struggle with is accepting that outcomes are not within your control. Instead, by recognising and understanding your current needs, wants, and desires you will allow yourself the ability to reflect on where your intentions lie: but you have

## HAPPINESS WITHIN

to be honest with yourself. Otherwise, you won't uncover the meaning behind your actions. Beneath this inward reflection is a journey of self-discovery towards your personal happiness. You will uncover your own personal levels of happiness, as well as how you can replicate it, despite everything going on around you.

*They say a person needs just three things to be truly happy in this world: someone to love, something to do, and something to hope for.*
Tom Bodett

Now whenever I recall moments of happiness in my life, I realise they were always etched into my memory because of times I was truly in the present moment. It could be that we are asking the wrong question. Martin Seligman suggests instead of asking 'how can I be happy?', we must first make a distinction between what pleasure is and what gratification means to you.[3]

Eventually, I was able to experience or even cultivate completely uncontrived moments of pure happiness. Moments that were not manifested because there was a moment, an occasion, or good news that put me in a state of fulfilment. It would be an experience of delight, peace, happiness, being in the moment, and enjoying my surroundings. An example was when I would be driving to work. Within this everyday task, I took in the journey. I observed the things around me and began to be mindful of those experiences. Things such as the sun's rays seeping through the windscreen, kissing my skin with a warm glow, or taking in the subtle dance between the tree leaves as they hummed to their own beat sung by the summer breeze. The music from the radio would caress my heart and soul, or sometimes I could be taking in the silence within the surroundings on my drive before I would begin my workday. What I did not know back then was that those moments were created by habits I would use in the future. I could draw in my surroundings and allow it to ground me in that moment. Within those moments nothing else mattered: my attention stayed present, and I experienced joy and happiness.

## TIME TO CONSIDER

Find a quiet place to sit and reflect how you are feeling. Get a notebook and pen to write down anything that comes up. When I first began writing, it helped me navigate the circumstances in my day. I tended to write whenever I felt called to. As the years progressed, I used gratitude as the main theme and practised intention setting to guide my writing. Sometimes I would set an intention for the following day. Another method is to simply listen to your heart and let your fingers hover over the keyboard, over time I found typing on the laptop kept up with the pace of my thoughts. Write what you are feeling; there is no right or wrong way. Each day may bring you different lessons and this is a way to access and find clarity around your thoughts and feelings in a judgement-free zone.

It may happen straight away, or it may take a few days. I suggest you repeat this exercise every day for 14 days. This is a simple observational exercise and must be written down because you will most likely forget on day 8 what you felt on day 1 – similar to how many people will not be able to tell you what they ate 14 days ago.

The key in this exercise is to be patient with yourself. While some things may be obvious, the process of writing things down can bring up things you had not thought of before. Putting things on paper, or writing on the computer, will gain you access to another perspective and understand what your personal process is. This will provide clarity.

A client once assured me they did this exercise but did not write things down. But the purpose of the notebook and placing pen to paper means you are unlikely to go through a distracting thought cycle. Once you write things down you will begin to clarify your thoughts, whereas when you ruminate, your thoughts can remain fragmented and scattered. You will be able to identify patterns, see connections, externalise thoughts in order to create a healthy distance, and allow them to form tangible observations, rather than getting caught up in your emotions. Writing things down is also therapeutic, particularly when emotions can be complex and overwhelming. You may also begin to weigh pros and cons, a reference point in which you can revisit and foster personal growth, as well as self-awareness over time. Once you have written your thoughts and feelings down, you are able to see it from a different perspective. The written format enables you to pause, re-read, and reflect. Thoughts may become erratic, they may often lead you to attaching yourself to other thoughts or new ideas – and they can distract you from the purpose of the activity.

Think of thoughts being similar to clouds in the sky: you observe them as they pass by. The purpose is to clarify your interpretation and enable you to develop your thought process on a subject. Identify things that may cause you feelings of unhappiness or upset, as well as feelings of elation or joy. You may be someone who blocks chances for emotional intimacy in relationships (this could be within friendships or romantic partnerships). Identifying your thoughts moves you closer to what you do want. I used to have thoughts that I didn't want a relationship and that I was happy or fine on my own. To some degree this was true, but the awareness and self-reflection gave me the comprehension that the underlying reason I kept using was actually a lie and became a mere excuse to block people out from being close to me. The use of journaling enabled me to release any hesitations and reflect upon my innermost, personal desires.

It is important to not judge yourself in a moment of pure vulnerability and acknowledge the space you have created to be open and honest with yourself. The final point is that delving deeper into your desires does not mean you need to take action just yet. This is a simple method to raise awareness into things that may be troubling you; things you may have resisted in order to stay in that unproductive middle ground and reduce your state of happiness.

If you are new to journalling, you may find this exercise useful. Grab a pen and paper and write down answers to these questions on the following page.

1. **What does happiness look like to you?**

2. **What brings you joyful moments that do not last long (short-term pleasure)?**

3. **What brings you content and happiness when you look outside yourself (gratification)?**

4. **Which things bring you happiness during the day?**

5. **What are you gratefully happy about in your life today?**

6. **What does happiness mean to you?**

In time, this may be the turning point you need to realise everything you need and want is around the corner, but only once you are honest about what that really means to you.

## CHAPTER THREE: WOES OF WORRYING

*Worrying does not take away tomorrow's troubles, it takes away today's peace.*
Randy Armstrong

We all have mental chatter running through our brains, whether you are aware of it or not. It's present during every second and every minute of our waking day. That inner voice we hear is our very own commentary team: they attend each event, participate in every conversation, and are present in everything we do. We experience around 60,000–80,000 thoughts per day: those thousands of ideas, opinions, and views are estimated to be 2,500–3,300 thoughts per hour! Our inner dialogue plays a significant part not only in current and future decisions we make but it also emulates from our experiences.

Each day around 80% of those thoughts are negative and 95% are repetitive. This implies much of what we think is not new; they are regurgitated thoughts. Thoughts that we may have pondered on the day before and the day before that. Within our lifetime, this commentary team navigates us throughout our day. The cells in our brain are active and the term 'cognitive space' refers to everything we encounter that has physical properties. We are prone to naturally organising everything that is in reference to our knowledge about it. This means our mental chatter, or commentary team, consistently labels everything we see. We are prone to this habit in order to understand our environment, remembering mistakes in order to avoid repeating them, or adding logic to our circumstances.

Take, for example, a simple task of looking out the window observing a man walking his dog in the rain. Using your inner dialogue to narrate this picture, you may start to use your judgements and past experiences to add more content, and context to what you observe. For instance, you question, *why isn't this man wearing a jacket? He's only wearing a T-shirt whilst it's pouring with rain.* Suddenly you begin to question the person's judgement and then their character, without uttering a word to them. You may take another route and focus on the dog: the coat, the size, or breed. It may remind you of your friend's canine and your thoughts take you on an exploratory adventure. You will end up elaborating on the picture in front of you via your previous knowledge and past experiences, as well as your intellect; all of which give you parameters for a story without any clue about the person, their character, intentions, or circumstances. Those thoughts create a narrative in order for you to comprehend something in front of you. All because of having this internal commentary team which describes everything you are seeing, and as a consequence you label things for your understanding.

The cells in our brain create patterns because our brain loves regularity. This cycle imprints in our memory bank and forms a mental map of our surroundings that will be stored and reactivated during later visits. Regardless of the substance of our thoughts, we allow this train to pave a pathway within our mental capacity, and we are able to make inferences about new objects and situations. Take, for example, making judgements about an animal. Although you are unlikely to encounter a lion in your waking life or existence, you still have the understanding that this creature belongs to the feline family, it is a wild creature, and quite ferocious. This knowledge is within your cognitive space allowing you to generalise on novel situations. You know if you saw such a creature in real life, you would be in danger because they are savage and could threaten your life. Your knowledge infers how you would behave as well as act should you face this animal.

However, as you are less likely to come across such a creature, let us refer to the pattern our brains make in everyday events for a clearer comparison. As stated above, you encounter around 60,000–80,000 thoughts per day; many of them are unconscious. Thoughts and emotions can easily be intertwined and confusing. But thoughts and emotions are not the same thing. Your emotions give you insight whether what you are thinking is generating a positive or negative response throughout your body. Since your body holds on to these emotions, they will influence your choices and decisions you make each and every day. Should you find your thoughts dwelling on the past or distracted by your future, you should know it is actually your emotions that have triggered reminders and will instigate your motivations. So if you are in a negative emotional state, your choices and decisions create and reflect that state back to you. This will be automatic, unless you shift your emotions. This is especially true for those who may be battling fear, guilt, or worrying about things that may or may not happen. Our brain is drifting between realms of fantasy, fiction, and negativity. Within this multitude of thoughts, there are thoughts that allow us to focus on the important things and that includes focusing on the present moment.

The question is, if many of our thoughts are unconscious – and often negative – and we are constantly obsessing over the irrelevant, how can we change those particular thoughts? How can we navigate the thought so that when we spill our coffee in the morning we do not latch it onto another bad event, or allow it licence to create a negative day? How can we rewire the process that has served us all these years and prevent negative, repetitive thoughts, which can be debilitating as well as self-sabotaging?

There were moments in my life when I failed to acknowledge such internal chatter. After all, haven't we all been told if we hear voices we are going mad? Have we not been conditioned that this is a sign of a mental disorder? Therefore why would we share this experience to the world? It's important to clarify that we *all* have an inner voice. I know friends who talk to themselves when going through a difficult task. We use the term 'thinking out loud' as it clarifies thoughts whilst carrying out a job. This voice is also our internal interpreter; we may not need to verbalise it, but we do. Years ago, during my time working as an area manager, I saw this fantastically demonstrated by my colleagues, which led me to do it more often. That was also around the time I realised my inner dialogue often incited self-sabotage, criticism, and worry. When this worry became incapacitating, I sought a solution and came across a book from Dale Carnegie called *How to Stop Worrying and Start Living* – this self-explanatory title was exactly what I needed.

Since I considered myself an expert at overthinking situations, overanalysing events in my past, or agonising about upcoming scenarios I wanted support on how to change this thought pattern. Did you know one in four people will meet the criteria of having an anxiety disorder at some point during their lifetime?[1] Worrying is a special form of fear and it affects our cerebral cortex. We can be specialists when it comes to fear and worry because we allow it to be complex by adding anticipation and memories to our own convoluted imagination, and we strengthen this by tagging it onto our emotions.[1]

Now that we have the knowledge and awareness that thousands of thoughts are mostly negative, it is important to understand we are not alone. It could be that lack of awareness means we do not pay any attention to this dialogue within our head. Our commentary team allows us to gather momentum on thoughts, which becomes enhanced by our imagination and then we boost this visual into 3D by adding emotion. Let's illustrate this by labelling 'emotion' as an attachment. Attaching to a particular thought strengthens our brain's wiring into a long-term memory, like an electrical charge. Each time you focus your attention on that attachment, it generates more energy. For instance, when you relive an argument with a friend or partner, the same thoughts and emotions transport you back to that very moment in time. This momentum is multiplied each time you focus on the memory; suddenly it has developed and converted this energy into a stronger current.

A simple exercise will provide you with an example. Imagine you are having the happiest day in your life and then you think back to when you were utterly devastated, heartbroken, or disappointed. Do you remember how much pain you were in? Suddenly this recap will drain the happiness out of your current state and you find you are replicating the emotions you felt on that painful day. Your physical body will also change in response to your feelings. Actors use this method when they are performing an emotional scene; it's called emotional memory technique. An actor will recall a real experience from their own past, where they felt a similar emotion to use those feelings in the role they are playing.

If we succumb to our internal chatter (worse if we are unaware of it) we are not able to control where our thoughts travel to nor are we able to control our emotional attachment to it. We have generated this superpower that allows us to feel hard done by, sad, and/or victimised through our past experiences.

Simply by worrying and thinking about something that upsets you, your body will react. Your autonomic nervous system is on high alert, your pulse raises, your blood pressure increases, and your breathing is short and shallow. That thought may have originated weeks, months, or years ago, yet when you remember the circumstance or event you bring with it the same emotional attachment into your present existence. Each time we relive the event, we generate more energy and therefore strengthen this attachment to the familiar feeling. We draw it closer to us, we are even protective of it. We may even convince ourselves with thoughts such as, *No one else is going through this ... No one else knows what it's like ... Nobody knows what I'm feeling* ... because we like to sustain the individuality of our experiences.

With the lack of control when it comes to our thoughts, we are placing ourselves within the mercy of that negative state. This state is often something no one else can bring us out of, even if we wanted to. Suddenly, we feel attachment to this event, we label it as a characteristic of why we act the way we do in certain circumstances and may use this to describe our trauma as simply a part of who we are now. Some of us may feel deeply scarred by a previous experience and some may be holding onto their victim story. If we are not careful, such stories are eventually used to define who we are as a person. Some end up suppressing this as anger and the only outlet they have is to mistreat others. They relieve their own pain without taking responsibility for the actions and behaviours they've adopted because of the lack of awareness or ability to leave it in the past. These can be the extreme consequences of letting a thought evolve into something bigger that affects our every decision we make now, and in the future.

Another example is if someone has been hurt in a past relationship. This hurt can cause them to feel extreme negativity when embarking on a new relationship and those previous fears and thoughts of harmful consequences remain. They may generate assumptions about the new partner because of their past trauma, such as, *They will cheat on me ... They will hurt me ...* or *... They will leave me.* Suddenly a person's comments or actions are being fed into the worrying thoughts of fear, anxiety, and sadness because our brain refers back to those patterns it is familiar with. Constant repetition of these negative thought patterns puts more and more energy into these thoughts and events, and

that particular neural pathway is strengthened. By repeating our own story and only seeing the negative we are giving it more attention, more momentum. We are missing the bigger picture, causing us disabling panic, anxiety, concern, and unease.

The key thing to understand is that while there will always be some level of challenge in our lives, we can choose in which state we carry out these challenges, and overcome them. For many people, there is a constant worry, yet worrying is insidious, invisible, and it leaches into anything drifting through the mind. Worrying is often associated with experiencing negativity, which prevents you from being happy. You may also find difficulty in accepting and enjoying your achievements because worrying prevents you from experiencing these. Worrying causes you to consistently place concern and fear upon things; it brings with it an undercurrent of pessimism and this causes needless suffering, taking away your peace of mind.[1]

There are studies that suggest certain people are prone to stress because their brain is less sensitive to natural stress modulators, yet there is scope to adapt and be flexible enough to redirect, retrain, and reset those neural pathways. By taking control of these stressful situations, it is possible to reduce the levels of worry certain individuals may be susceptible to. As noted above, worries can stem from previous experiences and then maintain their presence in future events through those neural pathways.

Becoming aware of thoughts is the initial key. Think of a thought as a train: you are the driver and you are controlling the thought train, you are in control of its journey, you decide what action to take before it gathers momentum and leaves the station. In your previous and regular brain patterns, you are used to taking the same train, which takes you on the same journey to the same destination. Awareness of thoughts will strengthen your capability to redirect the train into a new experience, a new journey, and a new adventure. Through awareness alone you are already bringing back a level of control regarding your thoughts. This awareness will allow you to be conscious to which emotions and feelings those thoughts have brought up for you. When you navigate thoughts into the present moment, you can allow for a new journey to take place and consequently will have the ability to experience new things. Think of this as creating a split in the train tracks – especially if your thoughts have gathered momentum and left the station – a new diversion (a new track) is presented for you to take, thus you are bringing awareness to the original thought and redirecting it towards a new route and a new experience, but *you* must be the one to create the diversion.

You might be thinking, *What can be done and how can I redirect old thought patterns into new ones?* When you are taking the same train to the same destination, this has given your brain a regular pattern which it is accustomed to; this is a strong circuitry connection. Therefore, you will need to bring awareness as to what the pattern is before you change it. This change will require you to replace the thought (before it gives you the same feeling, the same emotion, and same reaction) and redirect it into a healthier alternative. It is much like replacing an old habit with a new, much healthier one. However, this will not be an easy task. It can be a lengthy process.

The good news is that awareness is the first step. Once you observe yourself, your thoughts, and patterns – particularly when such negative thinking occurs – you are acknowledging your current route and noticing any familiarities on recurring thought patterns. This exercise alone will give you a chance to become self-aware. Once you have begun to establish the awareness of thoughts, your next step is to halt the train before it gathers speed. At first, you may find your thought train has picked up pace and it will be difficult to divert it onto new tracks. You may find you gather momentum as you begin to relive the same experience, emotions, and feelings from your past. It may be a pattern of fear you are reliving; a fear of something that may happen in the future. This future fear brings a sense of anxiety, stress, and worry into your present state. It is important to observe the possibility that you are holding on to a path because it is comfortable and familiar, and that you can decide to let go of those old patterns – but you have to be willing. This part of your journey is where you detach your personal emotions from your thoughts in any given situation. The first step is acknowledgement, the second is detachment, and the third is to change the thought.

After acknowledging the thoughts that come with certain situations, you may feel extremely uneasy detaching yourself from them. On an unconscious level, some individuals are familiar with these thoughts and find them strangely comforting. Your inner critic (or commentary team) actively plays the victim card. Accepting where you are now – without judgement – is a big step before you move to changing such familiar habits. You may be someone who is unaware of this; if so, having close allies may prove to be a helpful tool for you. It could be beneficial to choose a close friend or family member and make them aware of your intentions: ensure you are specific and open to what they might say. Most importantly, try not to become defensive. Now is your time to embrace change before you create a new journey.

For me, I found a familiar pattern in the 'what ifs'. I would conjure up negative scenarios about situations before they occurred, and this prevented me from acting and enjoying the current moments. It would be debilitating because I was anticipating something I feared would come true. At the time it became a familiar merry-go-round. Worrying about potential, horrible events in the future brought me nightmares and consequently affected both my current and future chances in forming new relationships. Other negative scenarios filtered into my professional life which made me worry insidiously and prevented me from taking risks. Those thoughts led me to scenarios where I would form logical justifications that prevented me from taking any positive action. Those fears eventually manifested into a physical form where I was attacking my own body from the inside.

When I had triggering thoughts about the future, they would bring me fear, stress, and anxiety in my present state. My body would react by breaking out in allergic reactions, I'd suffer from severe cramps, and I would gain weight: I couldn't understand why I was suffering physically. At that stage I was still unaware of the reasons why I would worry and what the patterns causing it were. Occasionally I had panic attacks. I was eventually diagnosed with irritable bowel syndrome (IBS) and developed certain food intolerances that all affected my daily life. At the time, I felt as if my worries were valid. I let my inner dialogue predict my behaviour and withdrew from being happy, which led me into self-sabotage mode.

Anything we pursue will not lead to happiness if we take our past turmoil with us. By derailing our old thought patterns and silencing the inner critic, you are leading the pathway into a space that cultivates inner happiness and peace. In a world full of distractions we are used to ignoring our thoughts and feelings and we silence the voice that is crying out for help. The world we live in shows us examples of what to do, what to feel, and how to act. We are taught what to enjoy, what to strive for, and are told what happiness should look like. Yet, everyone is different: this is a key moment to look inward and discover what it is lying underneath, what is causing *your* unhappiness. Clearing out old patterns and cleaning the closet where you keep things hidden gives you a crucial opportunity to discover what it is you are regurgitating in your mind and understand why it is there.

Take a moment to be present, in this very moment, literally right now. Wherever you are reading these words, acknowledge it. At the end of this paragraph, I'd appreciate if you can put the book down and take a pen and paper to write down all the things you have accomplished and all the things you are proud of in your life. List at least ten items (or more, if you have them). Use this moment to acknowledge and appreciate yourself: create a list of all the things that have brought you happiness. It should bring you into a space of contentment and peace. Now if you can change your mindset into a positive, content, and happy space in an instant, imagine recreating that every time you face those negative, worrying thoughts.

Once you have taken time to acknowledge everything you have accomplished, think about writing down how committed you are to your family and friends.

**What qualities do you bring into a relationship, or how dedicated you are in your job?**

Maybe include how you are expanding your personal development (including reading this book) allowing you to thrive to be a better version of yourself to yourself and to others.

Take this moment to notice everything you have done, up to this point. Include everything that has brought you here; including all the rough lessons you have learnt.

When holding on to worry, it manifests itself into emotions such as disappointment, anger, and frustration – to name a few. We may hold on to a grudge and lash out at strangers (or worse, our loved ones) because we are stuck in a cycle we keep replaying. As a result, we are not appreciating where we are today; we are holding on to old baggage that has passed through time.

Whenever you are feeling those anxious, upsetting emotions it is usually because it is taking you away from acknowledging how far you have come and appreciating where you are now. This worrying mindset is preventing you from keeping your gaze fixed forward. The reality is this is only one moment in time. It is one fraction of your whole existence here on Earth. Nothing is permanent and only you have the option to move forward towards the things you can control. Gathering things to be grateful for – particularly the things which have brought you here – means you can choose to keep using that momentum to continue to move ahead.

The inner critic may fixate on conjuring up worst-case scenarios. You obsess on your past trauma, the hurt it has caused you, and you refrain from taking further risks in the future. Maybe you have been cheated on; this hurt prevents you from trusting another person again and you take fewer chances in dating or meeting someone new. You may sabotage relationships before they cause you hurt and pain in the future. All these worries open old wounds, they stop you from taking risks, and they dictate the way you think about your future, discouraging you from believing in your own capabilities. This worrying and/or fear is deeply rooted in your unhappiness and prevents you from unlocking potential happiness moving forward. What if you missed a huge opportunity because you were scared? If you have taken a few shots and failed, then what? Do you quit and say it wasn't for you and move on to the next thing, or will you keep shooting for the goal and refine your technique? The question is: will you keep trying?

Wayne Gretzky, also known as 'the Great One', is considered to be the greatest hockey player of all time. A six-time All-Star shooter who holds 61 records to his name! No other player in the league has scored 200 points in one season. He did. Four times. His famous quote is:

*You miss 100% of the shots you don't take.*
Wayne Gretzky

If you stop shooting, you will never get to the goal. The best chance for you to get to the target is to keep shooting, to keep trying. You may be like me; that you fear the what ifs and therefore take fewer chances because you may fail or get hurt. Or perhaps you are afraid of what others think.

You are what you think. Your inner commentary team will keep repeating the stories that are familiar to you. But now is your chance to improve it, change it, and move on from it. Every failure is an opportunity, because when you fail you learn you have a better understanding of how to do it differently next time.

If you have experienced a string of bad relationships, will you give up and not try again? Unless being single is a personal choice, would you be willing to put yourself out there to find happiness in another relationship? Have you begun to understand, from the failed relationships, everything you do not want in a partner? Have you undergone personal growth that allows you to be a better partner? The point is to understand it is difficult but essential to step outside of your headspace when there is a cyclone of negativity because that is what narrows your perception. You are imagining countless scenarios for potential failed outcomes and these play into your negativity cycle because you keep pressing replay. Anxiety creeps in and prevents you from trying again: you invited it in to sit and ponder and divert you off your path.

If the above mindset continues, you will always allow your personal insecurities to discourage what you genuinely want, desire, and aim for yourself. When worrying turns into anxiety, it turns into suffering and can lead to physical pain like the ones I shared above. You may be debilitated by fear and panic or feelings of losing control. You may encounter feelings of being hijacked; your body no longer feels somewhere you belong, and it is no longer a safe place because you've invited worry to manifest into something bigger than it originally was.

Worry and fear amplify stress within your body's nervous system: you may experience rapid breathing; your pulse increases, and accelerates your respiratory system. Your body is responding to the fear you feel and is manifesting it as panic and anxiety as if you were physically running away from danger, when realistically, at that very moment, there is no danger in front of you. When you have thoughts of panic, fear, and anxiety, it is important to have tools that bring you back to the present moment. To remind you, you are safe. This is something to remember when re-enacting those worries you are familiar with. Your fight-or-flight response is a clear demonstration that your body has raised its alarm bells. You may find it is rarely focused on a singular topic or issue: it can manifest from a series of anxious moments, thoughts, or feelings from the worries you have been brewing over time.

Therapy can be a terrific solution for some – it didn't work for me but it can work for 60 to 80% of participants. Therapy is a great tool for individuals to become aware of what is causing this worry, what you are holding on to, and understanding which solutions are best suited for you. Instead of defaulting to escapism, letting the emotion in and understanding it before allowing it to flow through you is a great way to deal with the issues you may be facing. It took years to evolve into the person I am today. My personal wellbeing undergoes ever-evolving growth, full of perseverance.

*Every time you are knocked down and presented with a problem,*
*you are given another opportunity to get stronger.*
Tulshi Varsani

Another tool I used to redirect thoughts out of a worrying situation or negative state was to find out what the worst-case scenario would be. I used a similar strategy when planning a coaching session for an athlete or client. First, I would assess the goal or event my athlete would compete in, then I worked backwards to pave a way for them to reach this using relevant training methods. I then used this regressive awareness as a tool to navigate through a personal, specific situation. I would expand my problem and inflate it towards its highest peak, thinking of the ultimate worst-case scenario. It seemed daunting at first, yet this provided me with solutions and ways I could tackle the dilemma I was facing. This method heightened my awareness and gave me back control and power over the situation. It brought me back to reality because I took a more practical, problem-solving approach. I created an imaginary staircase, each step led me closer to expanding the problem, eventually it led me towards the pinnacle of the issue (the worst-case scenario) and this same staircase could then be used to walk away from it as I took account of the bigger picture. This led me to deescalate the problem because in its imaginary state things were not as bad as they seemed; I could also make it more manageable. Here is an example of when I used it.

A few years ago, I remember sitting in my room, crying. Nothing could settle me and I embraced the emotions of fear. There was no getting through to me and in time I fell asleep. My conscious worried state eventually subsided because I'd descended into a deep sleep. The next morning I woke up and couldn't shake the deep ache in my stomach.

A company I'd left had made additional payments into my bank account. I didn't fess up to receiving them but the company was now asking for the money back. I refused, stating because it was their error I assumed the money was now mine to keep. Now their legal team was chasing the money and I needed to face up to the actual problem and take action. I sat in my room and asked myself, *What is the worst-case scenario here? I have a buffer income but if this does not pan out could I go to jail for keeping what was in my account? Would I still have a home? Without the money I won't be homeless; I could still manage.*

*I could continue to fight this myself. I may need to go to court, pay for the additional expenses of court fees if I lost. I may get into debt if I fight for my moral high ground. I'd then be consumed with further worry and could potentially lose the case. This would also involve months of anticipation before a final decision would be made by both teams involved.*

*The other option was to take the legal advice given: do not fight and return the additional payments I'd received.*

*In the end, I decided if I let this go and settled I wouldn't be in debt. I would still be OK if I took the hit from losing the funds. This wasn't the worst thing in the world and ultimately my health was more important.*

Throughout this issue I'd sought advice from relatives; however, as mentioned above, seeking support from loved ones can make things worse because there are now more options to contend with. Advice can be conflicting, but the key is to find someone who understands you and gives you some objective guidance, particularly if you are incapable of making a clear, rational decision. Our fear takes our practical and logical decision-making abilities away from us too.

Have you experienced significant stress that caused you to spend hours lying in bed awake in the early hours of the morning? While awake in the small hours your thoughts began to manifest into more worry and anxiety until you found yourself on a rollercoaster ride you couldn't possibly get off; consumed by your own thoughts, all wasted energy.

If you have ever driven to work and not paid attention to the road because of the problems you are focusing on, that is the moment to wake up. Examples such as contemplating whether you will succeed in your business; deliberating whether your relationship will work out; or scrutinising whether you are doing the right thing in your job ... All this time being spent on those what ifs incapacitate your pursuit for action. All these thoughts in your mind have created a barrier and this barrier has now formed into a dam. A dam that halts your creativity, stalls your focus and attention regarding the present. The current moment is the crucial time – the only time – in which you can act. Yet fear, concern, and anxiety prevent you from taking action. Instead your barrage of thoughts, continuum of worry, anxiety, and time consumed in this state will lead you further away from where you need to be. Through shifting that momentum and diverting attention back to the present moment, you can act on creative flashes, instigate new ideas, create solutions to problems, and be open to new possibilities that arise before you. When you are concerned with problems, you miss opportunities right in front of you.

Have you ever been so upset that you fail to notice things around you? Worrying is similar to using a pocket torch at midnight. Your torch will only shine light on things you point it on. By focusing on the present moments, it is similar to the sun shining down on everything, illuminating your surroundings. This enables you to have 360-degree vision, to see finer details within 15 feet of where you stand. Through this clarity you begin to take action, problem-solve, and notice things happening.

## TIME TO CONSIDER

1. **When you are feeling anxious or worried, write down your feelings.**
   You may end up writing out the full scenario: that is OK because all of this will enable you to see your thoughts on paper and this can unload the burden you are carrying.

2. **Spot mental chatter and move away from it.**
   When you are aware of the mental chatter and catch yourself thinking negatively, navigate away from it.
   
   Should you feel you are speaking or thinking negatively about yourself and your situation and you find that difficult to spot, enlist a friend to hold you accountable. This means there is more than one of you to spot and divert the attention into something more positive instead.

3. **Catch yourself before you spiral out of control and it becomes paralysing.**
   Begin to change the way you speak to yourself. Replace it with things that are working for you right now. Stop yourself from replaying an event in your mind if you know it leads to an unhappy moment: think of a happier one instead. This will take some practice. You really need to focus and

visualise a happy moment in order for your physical self to respond to it. Another way to get into the habit of this is to count to 15. If you focus on your inhalation and exhalation, count the number of breaths you take in those 15 seconds; this should give you enough time to stop the thought train from leaving the station. This brief pause will give you enough time to jump onto another platform, one that is heading towards presence, joy, and happiness.

4. **Identify a list of things you can and cannot control in your life currently.**
   This is a great way to prepare to let go of the things you are unable to influence. In these eventualities you will be armed with knowledge of what is out of your control, giving you the opportunity to take steps to accept the things you cannot change and move towards the direction that is more productive, successful, and happier.

5. **Take a moment to think of the worst-case scenario.**
   What is truly the worst thing that can happen to you? If this is a work problem, is the worst-case scenario being fired? If it isn't, you have options. If it is, you can take steps to come to terms with the worst-case scenario and create actions that either prevent you from taking drastic measures or ones that allow you to rectify things with your manager or team.
   This method, despite the initial escalation, will ground you. It can be difficult to come back from this level of worry once those thoughts have gathered momentum but by taking the worst-case scenario and deciding on what potential issues may arise, you regain the power you may have thought you had lost. By attacking the problem and changing your perspective you will simultaneously drive yourself back to the present moment. Letting go of the need to control every eventuality will come with time, but having scenarios you know the answer to reinstates your control. This also means you can accept the current situation, plan for any eventualities, and focus on the moments that bring you back to the present.

## HAPPINESS WITHIN

Every time you try something you aren't good at and you fail, you get better than when you first tried it. If you stop trying every time and load yourself with what ifs, you will take away your opportunities for success. Successful entrepreneurs have one thing in common: they have failed at something. Every single person who has created something has taken risks. They ignored the what ifs and did not let their failures determine the way their life has gone. If you were able to overcome those what ifs, others would experience what you have to offer in this world. Whatever you have that is unique to you can be extended to others. Whether you have figured out your life's purpose or not, you have a choice to keep striving forward and ignore those worries and fears. By redirecting your thoughts, you are preventing the negative and unhelpful momentum building and refocusing your attention on what is working instead. Let it be your aim to stop that thought train before it leaves the station and gathers pace. Put your focus on doing what you need to keep moving towards your goals. Push aside the what ifs because they are standing in the way of your current happiness.

> *You may encounter many defeats, but you must not be defeated. In fact, it may be necessary to encounter the defeats, so you can know who you are, what you can rise from, how you can still come out of it.*
> Maya Angelou

## CHAPTER FOUR: WHAT IS HAPPINESS?

*If I had to give definition of happiness, it would be this: happiness needs nothing but itself; it doesn't have to be validated.*

Herman Koch

The Merriam-Webster Dictionary describes happiness as 'a state of well-being and contentment'. Happiness is a 'pleasurable or satisfying experience'. If this is the simplicity of what depicts happiness, why is it so fleeting? Are we experiencing lust and desire for something *we think* will give us happiness? Are we seeking happiness in someone or something that *we think* will make us happier and more fulfilled? Perhaps then only to realise that these are not the most sustainable ways to ensure happiness, as neither would result in the feeling leading to fulfilment or lasting joy?

How can we obtain the elusive state of happiness, make it sustainable, and thereby create a connection between happiness and personal success? What can we do to be successfully happy and how does that affect us in terms of our overall success rate in life? If we can identify what makes us happy does this automatically draw success to us, or is it that when people are successful they are happier? That is what I will reveal in this chapter: the definitions of happiness, success, and what it means to us. I will also touch upon theories and exercises we can use and do to have an increased state of happiness.

## HAPPINESS WITHIN

Modern society in the Western world supplies us with illustrations of what success and happiness is and showcases these by making us yearn for high income jobs. We see people who encapsulate success by dressing in designer clothes, living in vast mansions, owning luxury vehicles, and taking adventures to exotic destinations around the world. Our examples of success are individuals with fame and fortune. Society gives us permission and encourages us to validate ourselves through possessions. It is a marketing tool that has become increasingly profitable; something Henry Ford did so well. Not only did Henry Ford change the system of factory production, but he also increased wages for his workers who could then afford the cars he was making, and then he introduced leisure time for his employees. Collectively, the methods he introduced gave individuals the means, the desire, and the leisure to consume goods they were producing.

Over generations, we are spoon-fed the image of euphoria as a state connected to a material item: if we purchase something a celebrity or a sports person promotes, we assume we emulate that individual. Manufacturers play on audiences' insecurities to market their products, using scientific strategies to influence their marketing approach. The marketing industry's sole purpose is to makes us feel as if we can be better than who we currently are by reconditioning our thinking. A famous beauty company used the brilliance of messaging within their campaign. Their catchphrase 'Because I'm Worth It' was a strategy linked with supermodels. These models would showcase the brand and tempt their audience to take better care of themselves, via purchasing products. By the 2000s the company changed their slogan ever so slightly and also added tailored statistical research. These methods provided *scientific* knowledge to their users. (It must be noted that scientific research can contain many biases. Therefore it is important to consider who the target audience are and how many participants took part in any study, as well as if they are a part of the market shareholders within the company.) The change of just one word in their slogan 'Because *You're* Worth It' was phenomenally successful. It boosted their customers' mood, triggered feel-good emotions, and enticed women to showcase their worth through purchasing goods. Their mission statement is also extremely clever: originally 'Make Beauty Universal', which changed to 'Create The Beauty That Moves The World'.

These concepts of happiness are simply a notion of imitation. Consumers are sold on the idea that acquiring material objects can increase their levels of happiness; however, it must be noted that this state of happiness is always short-lived. We are drinking in the messages within our subconscious through media outlets such as magazines, adverts, and celebrities. These desires can be through a lack of awareness. Think back to a time when you have bought something because you may have been feeling blue. Or when going through a painful experience, such as a breakup, have you ever indulged in ice cream straight from the tub or consumed a whole bag of sweet-tooth goodies? This is highly common and a theme amongst many: people choosing to go shopping when they feel the need to increase their state of happiness and overall state in mood. When experiencing a negative feeling, you may have reached for a bar of chocolate to help fill that void when you are feeling down (I honestly don't know anyone who has craved a salad when experiencing a time of sadness).

Some individuals divert their attention by abusing substances such as alcohol, seeking to numb the pain of a bad experience to *feel better* in the moment. These are extremely harmful in suppressing emotions rather than confronting and processing them. You may have experienced a moment when you assumed this would help and allow you to feel better, even for a short period of time, but it usually ends up being worse when that momentary high is over. During that moment of sadness and pain isn't the time to reflect on your personal sabotages. But if you know you or someone else relies on diversion or avoidance, then seeking professional guidance to deal with such painful experiences is a good option to assess the underlying reasons for any triggers that have led you to experience physical or mental abuse.

Life gives us a series of ups and downs and many are conditioned into believing that there is no pleasure without pain. We may question ourselves and make misleading statements such as 'there is no such thing as being happy all the time'. This is incorrect: we can change our mood, outlook, and feeling should we choose to. We can find happiness in anything if we choose to see it. Happiness is found in loving yourself and loving others. And while happiness can also be found in the type of work you do, having a job or career does not necessarily accumulate happiness. For many, it may not be the sole purpose within their lives; neither does it drive their state of happiness. However, Amy Wrzeniewski describes people seeing their work as either:

- A job (focusing on financial rewards, as a necessity)
- A career (focusing on advancements) or
- A calling (the focus of enjoyment of fulfilling, as well as social useful work).[1]

The encouraging news is that there are various stages in which we obtain happiness and they are narrowed down to the following three types.[2]

**Type One**
As complex as it may be to pursue happiness, in its simplest form happiness can represent **joy and pleasure**, such as going shopping, laughing with a friend, listening to music, participating in your favourite hobby, and sex. All these examples come under the umbrella term of *happiness* because each of those examples can be joyful and pleasurable. However, these types of joyful experiences are short-lived and do not fulfil our sense of happiness for more than a fleeting period.

**Type Two**
Happiness is about our **personal wellbeing**; it will go beyond those momentary feelings that reside within the first type of happiness. Before I expand, take a moment, and ask yourself the following questions:

1. **At this present moment what is your current level of happiness?**
   Be honest with yourself. Rate it between one and ten: one being extremely unhappy, ten being extremely happy.

2. **How happy / satisfied are you with your life in general?**
   Rate it between one and ten: one being extremely unhappy, ten being extremely happy.

Measuring happiness will be explained further below, but it turns out it is very logical and profound. It is correlated with the measurements you can make on brain activity. It relates with many forms of behaviour. Using the answers you have provided is a great way to predict whether you will quit your job, end a relationship as well as predict things such as how productive you consider yourself to be.

This second type accounts for your perception of personal happiness. You should also consider how you compare yourself to others, as well as how you feel about your past. It consists of how we view our relationship with others, whether we are comfortable in the community we live in, as well as the work we are doing. In Scandinavian countries, the population is much less focused on the competition between individuals. Instead, they focus on the importance of finding things they can share with others, rather than showing how different they are.

**Type Three**
This type of happiness includes fulfilment on another level. Type three represents feelings of accomplishments of a higher meaning, as well as having self-actualisation. Maslow's hierarchy of (human) needs places self-actualisation at the

very top of the pyramid.† Therefore, this concept of happiness is much more difficult to measure than the previous two types. This stage accounts for more harmony on a deeper level, including what you consider to be life values. It is determined by how you would deal with inner conflicts, as well as resolving your personal feelings from your past. This level of happiness is aligned with the focal point of your very existence, and your contribution to the greater cause.

These three types are examples of gateways towards happiness. Undeniably, there is no one thing that will lead to a happier life, but the *culmination* of these three different types will increase your sense of happiness and fulfilment.

To summarise, happiness can be found in things and objects. It is also found in your perception of your happiness against others, and the connections you establish. Happiness will include doing good for others, as well as feeling internally fulfilled, whilst contributing to something bigger than your existence. Although we know there is short-term happiness associated with material objects, Socrates states happiness will not be via the accumulation of goods, but in the 'agency of the person themself who gives their life a direction and focus'. This was to insinuate that we must not satisfy our every desire but that we *should* determine which desires are worth satisfying through application via our critical and reflective intelligence.

The pursuit of internal fulfilment and long-term happiness cannot be achieved once we have reached a specific goal or outcome; this is futile. If individuals place happiness upon a condition, it will mean that (1) there is a need for it to be fulfilled and (2) depending upon your success and/or achievement rate, you will either be disappointed with the negative result or you will need to replace it with other goals once this has been achieved.

In simple terms, you will find no fulfilment in the ego mindset: this is where people insinuate that they will be happy

---

† There are plenty of examples of Maslow's hierarchy of needs available online.

once they have obtained an object or thing. Take the following as examples: losing weight, being in a new relationship, finding a different job, or receiving a promotion. All these begin with joyful and pleasurable experiences and feelings, but you will eventually revert to the same point your mindset was before you achieved that outcome. You may initially feel the thrill and excitement of wanting to achieve these goals, but once the goal is obtained, the lasting effects of joy and happiness can no longer sustain the levels of happiness you longed for.

If you are constantly trying to fill the void with statements such as 'I'll be happy when ...' or 'I need ... to be happy' you are planting the seed for an external outcome to manifest, therefore placing your happiness externally. As we stated earlier, this is short-lived and less meaningful.

You may be riding the wave of your current desire or lust for something that excites you, but this is ego-driven and superficial because when your desire or attention is diverted, you continue this cyclic effect of riding that wave of needs and ultimately it will not be satisfying in the long term.

In fact, it is our daily decisions and habits that impact our levels of happiness and success. We have come to learn through various studies that happiness cannot be achieved once the desire you long for is reached because you have already maximised its rate of satisfaction. Neither can happiness be obtained as a consequence of an event: it is and always will be about a state of being. The meaning and expectations of happiness have been obscured throughout the Western world. There are countless intelligently designed adverts which appeal to your superficial wishes and short-term needs, as well as your wants and desires. We are constantly bombarded with things that cling on to our senses or emotions, and these attach themselves to our perception of what happiness and success should look and feel like. These short-term yearnings give us what we think we need to be happy.

However, let me be clear, this is not a statement that in order to be happy we must be less ambitious or driven in what we desire from our life. Short-term and long-term goals are *both* beneficial in the pursuit of a person's purpose, whatever that may be. We can still aim for things we want in life but ensure we detach from the outcome. Instead of placing our happiness on the *outcome*, we pursue a state of happiness along the *journey* of our pursuit. We begin to set our own standards of success and happiness not as a by-product of achieving but integrating it along our voyage.

Shawn Achor found 10% of our long-term levels of happiness is based upon the external world whereas 90% of our long-term happiness is how the brain processes the world we find ourselves in.[3] This is extremely positive because it means we do not have to change our circumstances in order to experience happiness, and this emphasises that we have the control to change the way we perceive any set of given circumstances.

I always sought happiness outside myself: I was and still am extremely driven and ambitious. This made me goal-orientated and goal-centred, until I had a close friend remind me that I was allowed to enjoy my successes and achievements, instead of rushing towards the next thing. I was accustomed to constantly pursuing my next goal, the next phase. This was particularly evident within my career. I began to admit to myself that I was solely focused on the outcome; the biggest clue was that once I achieved that goal, it did not make me *feel* any different. Instead, I would be chasing the happiness associated with that goal without conscious awareness that what I was chasing was in fact elusive. I would be caught up within the passion and excitement I'd felt within my field of work, continuing to chase the goals, racking up the achievements or advancement in roles.

This illusion led me to believe that I was pursuing my personal happiness. My personal objective was entrenched in accomplishing training, achieving contracts, and gaining knowledge in furthering my education: all of which I defined as personal success, yet this also meant it wasn't ever enough. Inevitably, as soon as I achieved those things my goal posts would shift higher and further than they once were. As soon as I discovered that my purpose was to help people feel good about themselves, to offer tools to live a healthier, happier, abundant life, and to look after the body they were born into, my purpose carried me through times of difficulty.

Whilst my goal to progress remained in sight, I created a focused state within my current achievements which taught me to nurture and remain in the present moment, particularly when coaching. Within those instances, they provided a reminder that I can be fulfilled within the moment. Those moments grounded me and allowed me to revel in the journey. It allowed me to be absorbed in the individual or group I was coaching: nothing else mattered in that hour and the days would pass by quickly. During that time within those coaching moments, particularly later in my career, I found I would revel in those events that brought me that state of happiness. Those times coaching pushed me towards my purpose and immersing myself so I could continue to give my best. All the while, pursue success; I had simply found the meaning had evolved within that. This shifted my focus regarding my purpose. Instead of completely stopping chasing, pursuing, or making any plans towards my future, I stopped to smell the roses more often and appreciated the journey instead of focusing purely on the destination.

That shift in focus and perception is extremely important. Let's look at the example from Achor's study he conducted during his time travelling across the world. When Achor asked students at Harvard University in the United States of America whether they enjoyed doing schoolwork, his question was met with laughter or moans. However, when he visited Soweto in South Africa and asked the children the same question, their answer was completely different. Many of the children raised their hands in response to the question, stating they enjoyed participating in schoolwork.[4] This example demonstrates that the schoolchildren in South Africa perceived school as a privilege and they were fortunate enough to have schoolwork. The children knew their parents had not been as fortunate to experience this level of education for themselves, but they were able to pursue it. Education in Soweto was considered an honour and an opportunity to expand themselves and create a better future than their parents had been able to. In comparison, for the students at Harvard schoolwork is very often displayed as something of a chore because they are viewing it from their level of perception. I would hazard a guess Achor would have received similar, negative responses when asking students in the UK about their feelings towards schoolwork.

This makes a tremendous difference to the way you see everyday tasks and how much they matter to you each day: this is especially significant as it relates to your levels of happiness whilst you complete them. The great news is happiness isn't genetic; happiness is a choice. Despite our genetics or surroundings, we can choose to be happy now.

*Success is waking up in the morning and being happy.*
Unknown

Finding your own potential will allow positive emotion and cognitive awareness of growth.[4] In fact, your brain works best when you are experiencing such positive emotions. It triples your creativity, reduces fatigue, and there is evidence to show that happier workers have more success in their jobs. Achor describes happiness and health coming *before* success, not after.[4] He also claims success is a moving target, particularly in the modern world. Once you have achieved that goal, you need something else which fulfils that need which you labelled as success. For example, you may have placed emphasis on a particular project or job, you may say to yourself, *Once I achieve this, I will be successful.* However, if you are like me (or how I used to be), then when you reach that specific goal you may feel there is a need to fill that void, and soon you may find yourself moving swiftly towards the next goal. It can even leave you with a shallow feeling, as you are not able to enjoy that moment of success. You may be able to ride the wave longer than you initially expected but eventually that feeling will become hollow.

Have you noticed the trend in these examples of happiness and success? These empty feelings in happiness and success are fleeting as if they are outside of ourselves. Once we place a condition upon them, they will remain elusive and your expectation and circumstances not only become beyond your control; they now control your levels of happiness. This is where we ask, *How do successful people perceive their own happiness and sense of triumphs?*

Richard Branson described success as measuring how happy you are.[5] Arianna Huffington found many people see and associate success as having money and power. There is a third interpretation. Huffington describes success as having four pillars which are: wellbeing, wisdom, wonder, and giving. John Wooden describes success as being a state of mind. He described success as knowing you have made the effort to do the best of which you are capable of. Bill Gates believes success is measured via the people who are close to you, their own happiness, and their love towards you. Barack Obama states success is not how much money you make but the differences you can make in other people's lives.[5]

Now you may be thinking that it is easier to use these successful people as examples: they are happier because they already have money to support them and their desires. A study in Sweden surveyed 3,362 lottery prize winners who were monitored on their wellbeing between 5 and 22 years after they won the jackpot. Researchers found that winners who won larger sums of money (up to 2 million dollars) retained their wealth over a decade after the jackpot, but many did not quit their work. Instead, many had preferred to cut down their hours significantly and take longer vacation time. Also, the money they won did not seem to change their overall levels of happiness. When the subjects were asked questions such as 'do you laugh a lot?', 'do you smile a lot?', 'do you feel happy today?' there was no evidence that the lottery winners were happier in the long run, despite being more satisfied within their lives. Their state of happiness remained unchanged.[6] These results were generalised by the researchers who predicted the outcomes would be no different if the study had been conducted within the United States of America.

So how can happiness create the success we desire? Research from the *Journal of Neuroscience* found mood can affect our visual cortex processing. Subjects that are primed for positive moods process much more than those primed for negative moods. People who were positive made better business deals and this is also why organisations such as Google, Yahoo! and Virgin ensure their environments are fun, happy places to work in. Each time an employee experiences bursts of happiness, they get primed for creativity and motivation.[7] A Scandinavian country such as Denmark advances its work culture and has one of the highest rankings in world happiness reports. One of the reasons is thought to be a level of significant trust between individuals with a true sense of equality.[8] It is about trusting you are doing your job, receiving honest feedback, particularly when it can prevent misunderstandings and reduce office politics.

By being provided with an environment where people can express themselves, as well as receive the right to disconnect where they leave the office space, all these dimensions increase work satisfaction. It enhances the chance to filter this happiness into supporting individuals' work and personal life. This illustrates being successful does not make you happier but being happier and being more positive will enable you to be more successful (more on positivity in the next chapter). However, our personal rate of success comes down to what we class success as, what our perception of success is, and how we define this. The majority (75%) of success in life isn't about intelligence or success in this world; it's how we process this world and find deeper social connections.[3]

The most important thing to realise is we are not stuck with our genes or (for most people) within our current environment. Our perception allows us the freedom to choose to evolve our current state of happiness and how we live our lives through meaningful fulfilment. We do not need to identify ourselves as positivists, optimists, or pessimists; we can think in a much broader context. For example, scanning your current surroundings and choosing to focus your energy on what serves your purpose will trigger an electrical current. Should you choose to find happiness, fulfilment, and joy in your current state, it will give you the energy to pursue your goals.

Have you ever felt yourself experience a complete state of euphoria, whether it is spending quality time with your partner, hiking a mountain, writing your thoughts down on paper, or feeling the flow of working on a project you are fascinated by? All these will give you the energy to keep going. Those moments allow you to lose track of time: you may recall experiencing this type of flow when you unwittingly skip meals or become so completely absorbed in your work you forget to take a break. When you find this boost in energy, it generates more feelings of happiness. Let us not forget, should your environment or circumstance give you an emotion which you do not agree with, first you must assess what happiness means to you before you can change your perception.

## TIME TO CONSIDER

1) Define your current state of happiness: what does happiness mean to you, in your life?

2) What brings you feelings of joy and excitement?

3) How happy are you, really?

4) How do you compare yourself to others around you?

5) On a scale of one to ten how satisfied are you with your relationships with others?

6) How comfortable are you within your community?

7) What do you define 'happiness' to be?

8) What do you define 'success' to be?

9) List three things you can do each day for 21 days that increase your levels of personal happiness.

- ➢ One must include feelings that bring you joy/excitement.
- ➢ One must include being of service to others.
- ➢ One must include connecting to your deeper values.

None of these need to be costly. Examples could be:

- ➢ Watch an episode of your favourite television series.
- ➢ Send a heartfelt message to someone you love.
- ➢ What are your values? How can you encourage that in your daily life? For example, choosing to be consistently honest with someone despite any repercussions.

*Create a habit, practise that habit, and watch how much your day will change.*

Tulshi Varsani

## CHAPTER FIVE: TO BE OPTIMISTIC OR NOT TO BE OPTIMISTIC: IS IT EVEN A QUESTION?

*Optimism doesn't need to mean denying or avoiding negative events.
Instead, optimism is a mindset that we can cultivate that empowers us to cope with life's challenges.*
                                                                Unknown

If ever I was going through a difficult time, my mum used to give me this advice, 'It will be OK, it will work out' or if I faced rejection or disappointment she would say, 'Never mind, something will come up'. For a time, I was not sure what this meant, particularly because I would question how she knew such things would come into existence. I could not see how she could be so sure without evidence. Then the older I got, the more times I overcame disappointment and failures, the more times her advice reassured me, and the evidence was in the way time moved forward: things did, indeed, always manage to work themselves out.

Even though at the time I began to ponder whether my mum had psychic abilities, those series of coincidences where she would give reassurance and comfort through her words gave me the support I sought after, particularly when I was feeling defeated and vulnerable. There were moments when I really needed those words of comfort and I would crave them just to make me feel better about the situation. It felt good to have her level of positivity and confidence. Suddenly it occurred to me that she wasn't so much psychic; instead, it was her combination of hope, faith, and optimism, as well as seeing the bigger picture of life's challenges that provided comfort and reassurance. My mum had trust and confidence enough to know me and to have faith that this situation would not last and that this too shall pass.

At any age, humans tend to lean towards individuals who are similar to themselves. We are likely to identify with certain people, groups, and communities over others because of similar interests, goals, or hobbies. Some forge bonds through common things such as university studies, the area they grew up in, or the profession they are working in. When we identify characteristics that are similar to our own, we forge closer bonds to like-minded individuals, particularly with those who have similar traits to us, and we dismiss those who are opposite to us and our preferences. For example, a client of mine didn't see a future with a date because the guy didn't like mashed potato! To her, this was too absurd to even push past the feelings that may have run deeper if she overcame this specific food interest, or lack thereof. My point is the more things we have in common with another person, the more likely a bond will form. We enhance the relationship through increasing the time we communicate, as well as the way we interact with them.

Connections can also be manifested via our personality type. Whether we see ourselves as being pessimistic, realist, optimist, as introvert or extrovert (it's worth noting that opposites attract), the odds are higher when you have a variety of things in common and research has seen many individuals are hardwired to be more optimistic than not.[1] Optimism affects the wellbeing of a person's mental and physical health, as well as reducing personal stress. It is the belief that those who hold qualities of optimism tend to view outcomes and events in a more positive light. They see the outcomes of failure or negativity as temporary not permanent; they are specific rather than universal with their analysis and they are self-reflective. They also are accountable without tending to blame others for their failings. Optimistic individuals see the possibility for change. If you are leaning to one element of your character over another or if you struggle to be optimistic, how can you view life's dilemmas and situations in a more optimistic light? In this chapter we delve into relationships, success, wellbeing, and happiness, and their connections with optimism.

**Optimism and success**
Optimism allows us to persevere when times are tough, and it seems a likely factor towards long-term success. A study showed optimistic students were less likely to drop out of college and ten years later, they were also on higher incomes. It turns out the optimistic students had managed to persevere through challenges within the class or taken higher paying jobs.[2] It seems that when people assume good things will happen, they see the negatives as temporary hiccups rather than permanent disasters, therefore they are more likely to keep pushing through their efforts in order to pursue their goals. Having an optimistic outlook is effective when focusing on solutions rather than dwelling on the problems. It is on this deliberate focus that individuals remain optimistic and it allows them to remain within the present moment. Chemers et al. found that in college basketball, teams' performances were affected by the levels of optimism and confidence within their leaders and players. Both levels of confidence *and* optimism meant it would lead to better performances across the season, leading to their ability to succeed when it came to player performance outcomes.[3]

If you are an entrepreneur, you may naturally lean towards your optimistic side.[4] Having that type of characteristic will involve you taking calculated risks, despite continuous failures you may have experienced. Half of all start-ups fail in the first four years and 96% of businesses fail within the first ten years.[5] However, the outlook of these entrepreneurs is that they are far more optimistic about their start-ups and care far less about monetary rewards than those who earn a wage. Creativity is also another trait that is unleashed if you are an optimist. You may be able to create novel ideas for new services or products that have a greater chance for success. You may act whilst others question and deliberate for far too long. Being optimistic enables you to possess these elements that include risk-taking in order to succeed, instead of letting worry or fear deter you from your plans. Optimism means you are less afraid to fail. You can explore, stay curious, persevere, and keep reaching for success. This means unrealistic, optimistic entrepreneurs perform far better than realistic pessimists.[5]

**Optimists and relationships**
Optimists understand things are not permanent. The most certain thing in this world is that things will change; this very moment will never be again. If things are constantly changing and evolving, how does hope affect our levels of happiness? Well, whether we have hope or not depends on two dimensions. It involves finding permanent and universal causes of good events, along with temporary and specific causes for misfortune: that is the art of hope according to Martin Seligman's *Authentic Happiness*.[6] For some people, when a problem occurs, they can deal with the event and place it aside in order to move forwards. For others, the problem may haemorrhage into other aspects into their lives and thus create a bigger issue.

Take the example of a breakup. The person may have had their heart broken and they may make generalised statements such as 'I'm awful at relationships' or 'all people are cheaters'. This person may then begin to be miserable in work, they may refrain from socialising with their friends, and may even become reclusive in their daily life. This one event can spiral, causing further destruction in other areas of their life. Making universal explanations for failures means there is a likelihood to give up on everything. Being specific, however, means the problem is isolated and does not affect other areas of life. The permanence of this will affect how long a person will give up for. Temporary explanations are used to produce more resilience, whereas permanent explanations for negative events can produce long-lasting helplessness.[6]

Another example is someone losing their job. In this example, two people worked in the same company, as designers in a specific industry, both were given their redundancy notice. These two friends were also living with one another. As soon as their roles had ended there were clear differences on how each of them took the news, almost immediately. One friend began to question his identity. He was solemn and moody, irritable and sad. He didn't feel like getting up in the mornings and his self-esteem began to erode. He began to lose his purpose and he didn't know how to identify himself; his self-worth lay in the company and remained firmly upon the work he did. He began to shun people away, would reject offers of going out with his close friends and felt deflated. He would conjure irrational thoughts regarding his value within the team and the company, and he began to delve deeper into this world of negativity.

Conversely, his friend – despite being given the same news – kept the house tidy, she continued to keep up with the daily tasks. She continued to go to her yoga classes, kept up her daily training routine, and remained connected to her friends. She also remained positive and reminded herself that her job was not something she had to attach her identity to. By remaining optimistic she kept in mind an outlook of faith that she knew she would find something else better suited to her.

In this example a person's outlook ended up changing their behaviours because the news either ricocheted into other aspects of their lives, or it didn't. This is all dependent upon the person's outlook; whether they are filled with optimism and hopefulness or whether they remain in the mindset of negativity and feelings of victimisation. These after-effects from losing a job, or from any event or situation, can either be crippling or a chance to expand further; only you can dictate how long this phase will last.

It is said pessimistic individuals who get married are more likely to have a troublesome relationship in the long run. When couples give more positive explanations to problems or issues within the relationship they are more likely to create satisfaction within matrimony. Optimism allows for marriages to overcome things, particularly when your partner displeases you. More importantly, couples who are optimistic tend to be much happier and have an increased sense of happiness in their relationship overall. This is also true even if only one person is the optimist in the relationship. Optimists rarely see others as enemies and they try to see the good in everyone. They also tend to offer a benefit of doubt, meaning they are more likely to connect with others, in comparison to their pessimistic character types.

**Optimism and wellbeing**
Optimism affects physical wellbeing, especially in relation to cardiovascular health. It impacts mental health too. Optimistic individuals have a positive effect on accepting themselves and others. The levels of cholesterol in people who are optimistic are healthier than those who are pessimistic. Julia Boehm and Laura Kubzansky reviewed over 200 studies and there were clear links that demonstrated individuals with a positive psychological outlook were associated with reducing the risks of cardiovascular diseases.[7] In fact, the most optimistic individuals were around 50% more likely to have a reduced risk of experiencing cardiovascular stress, compared to their less optimistic counterparts. *Women's Health Initiative* found optimistic women had a 9% lower risk of coronary heart disease, over an eight-year period. Furthermore, optimistic individuals were less likely to die from all causes than those who classified themselves as being cynics. Women with higher levels of hostility and cynicism have greater chances of dying than those who had lower scores for hostility and cynicism.[8] A French study found men with significantly lower cardiovascular rates on 12 July 1988 than at any other time in history where women's rates had no significant difference. What was the reason? Well, France was in the FIFA World Cup final. This burst of optimism meant many French men enjoyed the lower risks of having fatal heart attacks on that day than at any other time that year.

Optimism is a large factor within mental wellbeing. Optimists cope with adversity and stressful situations and have increased resilience. They can problem-solve and handle negative information. One factor that explains the longevity of optimists may be because they are more likely to enjoy better health than pessimists because they lead healthier lifestyles. Optimists are likely to build stronger social support networks, they are more likely to exercise, seek better medical care, increasingly likely to live with their spouse, and less likely to smoke. Additionally, a positive outlook on life links to lower levels of cortisol, even when research takes age into account.[9]

My personal realisation was when I appreciated my natural state of optimism and how swiftly I was able to move on from any negative situation. This was a skill I treasured but didn't know how it had developed or how to nurture it because it came so naturally from a young age.

My dad would comment that I would get angry and argumentative as a teenager (tell me someone going through adolescence who is not a little volatile!). When I would get upset or angry, I would storm off to my bedroom, slam the door, and ruminate on my misery. However, the following day I would be totally fine; it was almost as if the previous day's event had never occurred. I woke up with a natural feeling that a brand-new day had automatically erased any residual anger. I began to understand I'd once had this natural ability to let things go and allow them stay in the past, where they belonged. Conversely, as an adult I began to allow my thoughts to linger and negativity would seep into minutes, hours, and days – far longer after the event had passed. This overriding mechanism of overthinking situations, conversations, and future outcomes was one aspect of my personality I soon realised was stopping me from taking chances. It was preventing me from being happy in the now.

Once I sought faith and clung to hope I used this optimistic state to narrow my vision. Instead of letting overriding negative thoughts take away my optimism, I clung to hopefulness; I started to change my mindset, and distracted myself from pessimistic reflections. Rather than being submerged into a destructive reactive state, I took steps to move forward in positivity.

There are some people who object to being positive: however, let me be clear. Being positive does not mean ignoring how you feel, distracting yourself from dealing with pain, anger, or harbouring resentment. Feel it, embrace it, then decide how long you want to dwell on it. That was the defining moment when I was a teenager: I was able to let it go. Rumination delays sleep, which meant as an adult I would cling on to thoughts late into the night. Yet everyone is individual and different. Only you know for how long you would like to avoid the emotions or hold on to something that hurts you. Only you get to decide what thoughts to think, what reaction you take, and how to act moving forwards.

Positivity is easy if it is a natural ability. I thought it was natural to me, until it wasn't. I needed to go back and find the optimistic, happy girl within me. This took time, effort, and attention. It is great to have all the tools at your fingertips, but you will only know if they have worked when you put them into practice and deal with a situation that will test you.

When a change is forced upon you, the shock effect brings up many emotions: you may not think about finding out more information, gaining clarity, or reflecting calmly on possible solutions. When you face an unexpected life event you follow your instinct. You may not have the chance to look inwards, seek to understand the situation and feelings, and perhaps find some clarity. An example, many people will experience, is a breakup. Should this happen suddenly it will come as a surprise to you and you may find it difficult to understand or comprehend in the moment. You may even never have an opportunity for closure. Yet within this new situation, you have choices: do you lock yourself away from loved ones and wallow in your misery? Do you embrace your friends and gain support for being a victim? You might create an opportunity to be physically active, move your body, and reflect upon the situation. In this last example you are moving on, despite a whirlwind of emotions; you are dealing with the upset through a healthy habit and thus creating dopamine for your mind.[‡] You are finding courage, optimism, and hope amongst a bad situation. You have found the good despite experiencing hurt and trauma.

---

[‡] You can read more about dopamine in chapters seven and ten.

Another example can be feeling lost, negative, or having anxiety about the unknown. For me, the black hole swallowed my optimism, particularly when I did not know what the outcome would be. Facing the unknown can be unnerving for anyone. You may feel able to choose an optimistic outlook, instead of worrying and fearing the unknown. These days, I am able to shift my perception to find adventures of possibilities that lie ahead of me instead of seeking random or undesirable predictions of my future. Positive predictions and manifestations are progressive in a person's life but if the situation leads you to constantly review a negative scenario, this isn't helping you in the short or long term. The more you replay the negative event, the more likely you are to keep telling yourself the same story and your body then reflects this feeling of disempowerment, disappointment, and sadness. This all prevents you from taking risks and moving forward.

Once I purposefully shifted my focus, chose to embrace faith, and trust that whatever the situation it will work itself out, despite facing the unknown (just as my mum always said), I sought to seek happiness within, looking for an excuse to seek happiness in the now and be optimistic and grateful about all the good that currently exists and potential for more to come. It took time but I shifted the way I looked at the situation. Over time, the rumination lessened.

*The strength of a woman is not measured by the impact that all her hardships in life have had on her; but the strength of a woman is measured by the extent of her refusal to allow those hardships to dictate her and who she becomes.*
C. JoyBell C

Wellbeing is an experience of health, happiness, and prosperity. As mentioned above, it includes good mental health, but it also involves life satisfaction, finding a sense of meaning or purpose, as well as having the ability to manage stress, something which is an inevitable component within life. Placing awareness on our daily habits and routines provides the perfect opportunity to change the patterns which would usually lead us to focus on the negative or the past. In time, this will lay the foundations for you to change your habitual reactions to stressful or unexpected situations. Setting habits in the everyday makes it more likely you will use those tools should unforeseen circumstances occur.

It was June 2016 and I was getting ready for a job interview early in the morning. It was for a high-performance company and this meant a great deal to me. I carried out my usual morning routine, deliberated my outfit, and continued to prepare as best as I could by revising potential answers to hypothetical questions. Although I felt as ready as I could be, this still didn't stop the sense of nervous anticipation creeping in. This led me to become distracted, causing me to spill my large cup of black coffee all over my make-up desk and onto the floor. This enormous stain was spreading in a pool on my cream-coloured bedroom carpet.

I swore out loud and began to get flustered. I started to generalise and amongst my frustrations (as a believer of fate) I chalked this mess towards being some sort of omen. I wanted to cry at my clumsy behaviour: emotions rose to the surface and I felt upset and irritated. I cursed myself because I'd added additional time before my interview; time I needed to clean the mess up; time I had neither contemplated nor accommodated for. I panicked because this wasn't in my plan and it ate into my preparations before leaving the house. I started to get increasingly angry at myself and negative questions invaded my mindset as I asked myself internally, *How could you be so clumsy?!*

Suddenly, I received a message from my dear friend wishing me luck. It was then that I turned to her for support and told her what happened.

'I spill coffee all over my desk all the time!' she replied. 'This is not a sign! It does not dictate how the rest of the day, or how your interview is going to go. Just breathe.'

She was incredibly reassuring and I did just that. I paused and tried to reframe my anxiety – which was solely based on the interview – and I reminded myself this one event would not dictate how the rest of the day panned out.

There were times I needed someone to remind me how to get out of my own headspace; other times I needed to talk myself out of the negativity that can so easily cause an avalanche of further upset and increase those angry emotions. I had let my thoughts spiral out of control and generalised the circumstances in an irrational manner. I'd become absorbed by panic and nervousness, which led to me turning a typical accident into something far bigger than it was.

It took time to bring myself out of those moments where I would spiral downwards and out of control; friends would often help when I opened up to them. However, the thing is, it is ordinary for someone to be optimistic and have moments like this crop up. There are times people justify occasions when something has gone wrong, when it can easily be related to other moments that increase our personal suffering. You host a party and no one turns up, there is a last-minute venue change, British weather rains on your BBQ, you wake up late, the wedding stylist isn't on time... It's highly likely you have experienced at least one of these scenarios, and even more likely one or more of them will happen to you in the future! At the moment of despair, don't forget to broaden your vision.

When I spilt my coffee, the small act of my friend texting me was enough to bring me back to the present moment and realise that the coffee spill – although frustrating and unexpected – had nothing to do with the upcoming interview or anything else I had planned for that day. It was an isolated incident and only I have the power to move forwards.

Some people live by a sentiment that bad luck comes in threes. Although this is not the worst solution to draw from a negative outcome (in a sense you can argue that bad luck is never your fault), it can often lead to further negativity creeping into your mindset. When you assume more bad luck is on the way, you anticipate the next 'bad' moment before it arises. Instead, you are allowing the hopelessness to seep into other aspects of your life and therefore allowing it to become a universal statement instead of facing the actual truth: the event or circumstance is standalone. Do not allow yourself to even anticipate another two unfortunate events arising. For your wellbeing, take it as it is and write off the original incident: put it behind you, and move forwards.

**Optimism and happiness**
Researchers have found people who have an increased sense of optimism are more likely to be open to new experiences and they are exceptionally predisposed to benefit from the activities that lead to positive reinforcements.[9] Having faith and trust in knowing it will all work out means you are taking on an optimistic stance without knowing the future. Once you realise that you can take yourself out of your headspace, you can use tools to eliminate any negative thoughts that arise. Those thoughts may tempt you into making the situation seem far worse than it is, but we know that no one can predict the future; all we know is that time will continue, life will move forward.

If we can increase our state of happiness by adding more optimism to our perception of things, we access chances to steer ourselves away from negative comments we hold in our own head.

➢ How can we predict that things can go well?
➢ Are we able to take negative moments as they are and allow them to pass by?
➢ Can we let our focus be redirected into circumstances that lead to more positive opportunities? Will we encounter more happiness and consequently more success?
➢ Are we able to experience more joyful moments and be present within our state of happiness by being more optimistic and writing off the negatives quickly?

### TIME TO CONSIDER

Melody was taking her children to school and she came across some traffic due to a road accident, and she knew this delay would make her children late for school and her late for work.

## Which of the two options below would you choose, if you were in Melody's position?

1) Think of the situation as someone has been hurt; it's lucky you and your children aren't involved; the school and your company will understand; this situation is out of your control. You take steps to call the school and your department in advance to let them know about the situation and consequential delay.

2) Panic frantically; beep your horn as you try to get out of this mess; let anxiousness fall upon you as you begin to imagine the children being marked as late. They may be embarrassed and judged going into school late and you will probably be considered a bad parent by the schoolteachers. Your work will pile up; you may miss the important meeting; you could be reprimanded for tardiness at work; this will affect your annual review and potentially the promotion and bonus you hoped for that year.

   ➢ Be honest with yourself, without judgement: what would you do naturally?
   ➢ Are you an optimist trusting everything will work itself out?
   ➢ Do you panic at the sign of change, convinced there will be a consequence to every action?
   ➢ Do you potentially overanalyse ways future actions could play out?

*How can I be more optimistic?*

1) **Focus on the solutions Instead of the problem**
   Think back to a problem and what your thoughts were doing in those moments. Observation is key here.

   ➢ What was your immediate reaction and response?
   ➢ How did that event make you feel?
   ➢ What were the emotions you encountered?

If you reassess that event, knowing what you know now, how would you have changed your response?

2) **Find a route for improvement on any given situation**
In the scenario you gave above, can you find any good within it?
   Take an example when someone has stood you up for a date or breaks up with you. Try thinking of this as something that has brought you freedom because they weren't meant for you. Something else that you can do after a breakup is look honestly at your shortcomings and work on them. Maybe you can chalk this up to a learning experience and it can push you further to success towards someone who is better suited for you, instead of having that relationship drag out for many more months or years.

3) **Be your own coach**
You have the capacity to be your own best friend. You can acknowledge your wins and appreciate the losses you have encountered in life; you know your situation more than anyone else on Earth. You owe it to yourself to be your best cheerleader within your team. Journaling can provide the opportunity to record ways in which you appreciate yourself as well as reflect on how you can optimise your successes and minimise your failures. Actively logging such lessons learnt from your experience will bring you awareness to your achievements. Your list can be specific or it can be general. Ensure the comments remain positive and uplifting; this will be useful when you are experiencing negative emotions.

4) **Practise positive affirmations**
When you think of a positive thought over and over, you are repeating statements that will gradually sink into your subconscious mind. For some, speaking statements which they do not believe initially will serve them well in their future. The purpose of this method is you will eventually believe those positive statements through repetition.

## 5) Change your inner dialogue

You may also see a difference if you were to change your internal commentary. This can be an effective tool to tackle negative self-talk. When you are aware of the words you speak or statements you generalise to yourself, you will be able to navigate it into a more positive or optimistic outlook. For example, take a comment such as 'I'm terrible at presentations'. You can change this statement to give yourself positive encouragement and instead you say, 'I am able to deliver a great presentation with practice, and I can do a great job through refining my technique.'

If you were to delve deeper into your internal negativity, you may try to understand what it is that causes you to think this way. Investigate those statements. For instance, taking the presentation as an example: you realise you may not like to be in front of an audience, you may feel pressure and/or anxiety when performing on stage. You may not know the material well enough, or you may lack the right tools to deliver an engaging presentation.

**Change your inner dialogue:**

- Look for the aims.
- Target the areas you wish to improve upon.
- Be gentle with yourself when applying these new skills.

This is a great way to focus your intention, support it via action, and lead using the approach to predict a positive outcome.

*By setting yourself challenges you will find answers leading you towards your path.*
*May you lead with the certainty and belief that it will always work out for you.*
*Lead with the determination that there is no other path but a successful one.*

Tulshi Varsani

## CHAPTER SIX: SHARE YOUR SMILE

*Peace begins with a smile*
Mother Teresa

Realising my dream job in an industry I'd adored since I was a child affected me in ways I never knew it could. In those initial months (before passion for the job became an unhealthy obsession) it seemed a given that living my dream working within motorsport ignited my passion and thirst for more knowledge. It was actually more so the surroundings that changed me. The environment provided me with a sense of community where I felt heard, understood, and comfortable being myself. That was when I flourished because it gave me access to expand my creativity, be vulnerable, and be open to new possibilities. Once I discovered my foundation, I began to feel at home with this new element of my life. I understood it was the people and the atmosphere that contributed to my overall levels of happiness. Two significant moments solidified this for me.

My usual morning routine included exercising first thing in the morning. Some days this would include the gym, other days it would be yoga in the living room. On this particular day, I decided to head into work early. It was 05.45 in the morning as I was walking through the race team's race bays and then the composite department.[§] There was a group of people on their shift cycle. For some it was time to go home, for others it was the start of their working day. As I walked past this department, I caught a technician's eye. We exchanged a smile and greeted one another with a 'good morning'. When someone offers you a warm welcome such as a smile or a hello, you can rarely ignore the invitation of kindness, even from a stranger on the street. Of course, for many it is polite to reciprocate a warm greeting.

Although I consider myself a cheery person, at that time in the morning even I can admit I hadn't fully woken up to my usual 'chipper' demeanour. However, I found even on those less cheery days, those moments were scattered around the factory across all departments and it truly lifted my spirits. I found the effects would flow into the rest of my days, weeks, and months following those regular interactions. It was this small but significant act of kindness that meant my day started well. It was the culture within the company, and it was then I knew it was more than a job. I had made it a home.

I can recall another pivotal moment when these interactions changed my mindset. I had finalised a relationship, and returning my key was my ultimate closure. I couldn't deal with this final blow and sensed it was the end of the road after countless times of going back and forth and getting nowhere. Feeling very emotional about the whole situation, I was in work and fairly new to the role, therefore I didn't know whom to rely on as yet. The factory wasn't small: I would describe it as being in a tiny English village that housed departments instead of families. The main reception area was in a picturesque spot: in front of it lay a beautiful stream flowing through a grassy embankment. It was a lovely scene, particularly on a summer's day.

That day I decided to take a short walk – in an attempt to gain some clarity – whilst breathing in fresh air. I strolled by

---

[§] Here they work on the chassis of the car. The introduction of a fibre reinforced chassis was one of the most significant developments in the history of motor racing: to this day they have continued to work on building the car chassis by hand at various stages of production.

someone who said 'hello'. It was a stranger, but someone whom I assumed worked there. By then, I'd understood this light greeting was common practice at the factory. I mustered my best brave face, forced it into a smile, and politely returned the greeting, despite having the feeling I would burst into tears at any moment.

The fact it was a stranger is what forced a false smile from me. If it were anyone else, anyone who knew me, they would have known I wasn't myself. It was then the thought struck me. That moment hurtled at me whilst I was spaced out and living in my own head. It brought me into the present moment and allowed me to bring awareness into what was happening now. Instead of going back to feeling downhearted, blue, wanting to cry, and feeling remorseful about the situation, I realised I could change my thoughts, in an instant. I could make the decision to remain in a low mood or focus on the now.

Something as simple as a smile, a 'hello', or a 'good morning' made the world of difference to me. It took me out of my headspace, it forced my attention away from my internal dialogue and it grounded me. Suddenly my focus shifted from the ending of a rocky friendship – where I was questioning why I'd failed, punishing myself on time wasted – instead that moment brought me back to the current reality of life. This present moment of being right here and now. That small but significant encounter suddenly transported me back to the moment I was living.

That was when I realised I no longer lived in my past.

Communication and interaction can influence states of happiness because they provide individuals with feelings of validation and acceptance. When individuals were evaluated, it was shown that happiness, in a social context, was important when identifying levels of happiness. Whether the person was native-born or a migrant, the evaluations presented strong evidence for connections and sharing institutions and social norms.[1] When the social norms meant a change in behaviour, it was then I realised within such tough moments, interactions can make the world of difference.

There is a saying:

*If you can be anything in this world, be kind.*
Unknown

This serves as a reminder that when you are feeling pain, anger, fear, or frustration you must be wary and prevent yourself from projecting those feelings and emotions onto others. Being kind to others prompts us to remember that everyone is dealing with their own issues or problems and by controlling our own outbursts and emotions we can remain in full control of our attitude and reactions – the ways in which this can be managed is detailed in the *'Zen as F\*ck'* chapter. Yet many people, sometimes without consideration, tend to offload some of their anger and upset onto others. It happens when the person has not dealt with something that has caused them to be upset. When you are going through something it can be difficult for it not to affect those around you.

When you are feeling a state of negativity or sadness you may notice it is contagious; it is the opposite but just as communicable as the example of smiling to a stranger. Smiling commonly indicates high levels of social interest and acceptance and is used to form bonds with others. It is of course more pronounced when people are engaged in social contact.[2] When we smile, neuronal signals travel from your brain's cortex into your brainstem, your facial muscles contract and there is a positive feedback loop; this reinforces your feeling of joy. Smiling stimulates your brain's rewards mechanisms in a way that even chocolate (a well-regarded pleasure-inducer) cannot match.[3] It seems when we smile, it gives us the same happiness as if we were exercising.

Participants in clinical tests were shown photos of family, friends, and loved ones smiling, or they were given money, or chocolate. Participants who were shown a child's smile experienced the same level of stimulation as they would have had from eating 2,000 chocolate bars or receiving 16,000 in cash! A survey found smiling creates a short-term high, ranking sex, chocolate, and shopping in that order *behind* smiling.[4] Powerful emotions are triggered when someone important in our lives smiles back: it changes our brain chemistry and creates a 'halo' effect. This helps us remember other happy events more vividly, causing us to feel more optimistic, more positive, and highly motivated.

The facial feedback phenomenon studied by Laird conducted two experiments manipulating participants' facial expressions, without their knowledge.[3,5] The partakers were asked to view cartoons whilst they were hooked up to electrode devices that were attached between their eyebrows, mouth, and jaw. Participants were asked to contract muscles at specific points and the theory was that if an individual's mouth was manipulated into the form of a smile, it would change their perception of a humorous clip.

When feeling low about a certain situation, I became aware that I was not living in the present moment. Mentally I was stuck in my feedback loop and I'd replay the negative event back – and these emotions had an effect on my body. It affected the way I carried myself, my demeanour, and even my posture. I was trapped in my head, my own perception of the event, and I needed to refocus my attention into the present. The consequence of overthinking meant I was holding onto something I no longer needed. As a result, this led to further anxiety, restless nights, and stress. When I was dealing with a work situation and couldn't sleep at 4 a.m. my brother once asked me, 'Is there anything you can do about it at 4 a.m.?' Suddenly it dawned on me: no, there is not. Ultimately there were two choices: start my workday that day early and answer emails, or rest, empty my thoughts on paper before bed, review my to-do list for the next day, and have a lie-in so I could be productive the following day.

Another situation allowed me to put being present into practice. After an upsetting moment at work, I was about to drive home, when I paused. This sudden awareness washed over me as I became conscious of my attachment to that negative event: I could feel the emotions brewing and that I was dwelling on them. It was then I decided I no longer wanted to recall and relive such moments; they were of no use to me. That was the moment: once I'd caught myself dwelling in the past, I raised my awareness and chose to change my feedback loop. On my drive home, I opted to *pretend* to place a pencil between my teeth, so the imaginary pencil would not touch my lips, forcing the engagement of my facial muscles, and consequently forcing my mouth to stimulate a smile.

There is a reason for pretending to place a pencil between my teeth. I'd remembered a study by Strack et al.[6] In the actual study Strack asked participants to hold a real pen in between their teeth – ensuring their mouth did not touch the pen – whilst they performed a task, which was to rate how funny cartoons were. This experiment found participants who placed the pen between their teeth rated cartoons funnier than when they held the pen with their lips (inducing a 'pout') Researchers suggest that 'smiling during brief periods of stress may help reduce the body's stress response, regardless of whether the person feels happy or not.'[6]

As that study came into my mind, I decided to mimic the action, quite dubious of it working because I still had the negative state of mind. However, I was adamant about pursuing a happier state, so I figured it was worth a shot and was better than the current mindset I was in. Despite contemplating how other drivers may perceive me, it took between 90 to 120 seconds for me to shift my mood from being upset and blue to feeling better – and for no other reason than changing my facial expression. I was transported into the present moment and felt significantly happier than I was before. I chose to change my state of mind through the action of my body. If I then chose to go back to those previous thoughts I would be taking myself out of the present moment. This changed my perception of how much I was aware of my feelings and emotions and how much power I had to change my state of happiness, whatever the circumstances.

Dr Niedenthal and her colleagues surveyed studies from brain scans to cultural observations in order to create a new scientific model of the smile.[3] The researchers believed they could account for the source of smiles, as well as how people perceived them. Pictures of salesclerks were shown to a group of students. Some of the smiles were genuine, some were fake. The students could tell the difference between them but when Dr Niedenthal and colleagues asked the students to place a pencil between their lips, producing a smile, they were unable to mimic the faces they saw (of salesclerks) and found it much harder to tell which smiles were real and which were fake. In another experiment, another group of students were shown the same clerks' faces. This second group could identify which were real and fake but as soon as they put the pencil in their mouth it wasn't clear which smile was genuine or false. So it seems while people can usually tell if smiles are fake or real, if you are smiling it doesn't matter how accurate our interpretation of another person's smile is; we feel good anyway. Despite modifying my 'smile' I felt the wonderous effects of what the study was trying to establish.

At this moment, pause, grab a pen or pencil and try this for yourself. Place the pen between your teeth and do not touch the pen with your lips. Maintain this upward motion for 120 seconds and reflect on how you feel before and after this mini experiment.

➢ Was your mindset altered? (Think how your mindset felt before you tried it).
➢ What did you expect to find from this change in state?
➢ Describe how you are feeling (i.e. maybe in a lighter state?)

Smiling changes our brain because of this feedback loop. As our brain tracks the number of times we smile, it therefore affects the emotional state we are in. Smiling reduces stress that your body and mind feel. Have you noticed being around children automatically gives you a sense of happiness? It is because children smile more than average. Children smile around four hundred times a day! Happy people smile around forty to fifty times a day, but the average adult only smiles about twenty times per day.

Smiling reduces the stress hormone that negatively affects your physical and mental health. *Psychological Science* published data by Ernest Abel and Michael Kruger, who rated smiles of professional baseball athletes captured in their 1952 yearbook. They predicted each player's age at death. In the end, all 46 players were still alive at the time of the study, yet the researchers showed that smile intensity can explain 35% of the variability in survival.[6] Another yearbook study tracked women who had the best smiles.[5] They found those who smiled most not only lived happier lives, but also had happier marriages, and fewer setbacks. Although studies have deduced correlation not causation, smiling can breed trust and make you happier and live longer. Krumhuber and colleagues found people who exhibit a smile (even if it is not perceived as genuine) are rated more likeable, attractive, trustworthy, and cooperative in comparison to people who assume a neutral expression.[3] The most important lesson here is this can be learnt and practised.

I allowed the moment when I was not feeling good me to raise my awareness to my physical expression and my internal mood and make an adjustment. I forced myself to smile and my attitude changed. Thinking of our outward behaviour allows us to be conscious to our thoughts. Before we navigate down a dark, rocky spiral of negativity, we can change our patterning by shifting direction, manipulating our physical demeanour, and as a result modify our mood. To re-learn how to smile genuinely and more frequently, try practising with some imaginative tools, such as the pencil or pen method.

Another tool is to visualise an event which gave you deep satisfaction and joy. This will require practice (meditation employs the use of this method). Using this methodology within your imagination allows you to visualise yourself in that moment. Similar to the exercise where you force yourself to smile, you are producing a neural connection and your body is responding to the joy you felt that day.

Guang Yue, an exercise psychologist from Cleveland, Ohio, compared results of those who performed physical exercises to the results of those who performed visual workouts.[**] The group that was physically active found their strength improved by 53%. The group that conducted 'mental contractions' via visualisations increased their strength by 35% without lifting a finger! The most surprising result of this study was that the greatest gain was not achieved until four weeks after the training was completed.[8] This is an important demonstration of how much the mind can provide power to your muscles and your body. You are training your brain via these mental practices that can enhance motivation, increase confidence, and self-efficacy. You are priming your brain for success.

## TIME TO CONSIDER[††]

1) **Reflective practice**
   When you are feeling a certain state or mood, it is easy to label that as a feeling. At times we can bypass its significance because we are limited by our vocabulary. When you are feeling a type of emotion, go deeper and find out what you are truly feeling. Perhaps describe the physical sensations instead of labelling that feeling. Delve deeper when you are describing these feelings to yourself, instead of the conventional 'good' versus 'bad' sentiment.
   Next you may sit and reflect *why* you are experiencing these things. Some of the answers may surprise you. They may lead you to an underlying issue you have not let go of or raise awareness to fears you are holding on to.

2) **Change your feelings**
   Now that you are aware of those emotions, you can take steps into changing those feelings. Firstly, be honest with yourself:

---

[**] A visual workout will require the participant to visualise themselves lifting and lowering weight as if they are actually doing the training without actually moving a muscle.
[††] Try doing this task when you are not feeling low. The best results will be when you are in a neutral state and can expand the variety in your answers.

- Would you want to dwell on this feeling?
- Have you formed an attachment to it?

You may be surprised that you answer 'yes' to this last question. If you are not willing to let go and change, you are using this to feed the negative state and play the victim (in some circumstances). If the answer is 'no', list ten things that make you feel happy instantly, which could include any of the below:

- Going out for a walk
- Listening to a song that always makes you smile
- Dancing
- Placing a pencil between your teeth

**3) Use your happy list**
The next stage is making sure that the list of ten happy things is readily available when you are feeling sad, frustrated, angry, disappointed, or blue. All these moments will define what you do next. To break the original cycle, you must do something different. By having the list of happy things to hand, you can choose any one of the exercises on the list before your negative mood or state declines further. Remember you need to rewire your brain's neural pattern before it becomes natural and easy. Everything requires a bit of effort and awareness when you first begin.

**4) Reflect on your self-intervention**
Now you can go back to reflect on how that intervention made you feel. Would you want to change your state and retreat to that unhappy moment? Or would you choose to live in the present moment, in this happy state where neither the past nor future affects you?

**5) Smile in the mirror**
My final tip is to look at yourself in the mirror and smile. Have you ever seen yourself smile in the mirror? Maybe put on your favourite uplifting song and practise smiling to

yourself. Give yourself a compliment and accept it. This shift will automatically improve your mood and reduce the stress hormones in your body; you will immediately feel happier and more relaxed.

*We shall never know all the good that a simple smile can do.*
                                                    Mother Teresa

## CHAPTER SEVEN: MY LOVE AFFAIR

I have fallen in and out of love numerous times in my life. I'm not talking about men or romantic partners: it was with training and the image I had of my body. I recall using exercise as a crutch to overcome heartbreak as I waded through the local leisure centre swimming pool, lap after lap. I attempted to find some clarity and quieten thoughts sprinting through my mind by pounding the roads before sunrise. I sought solace in weightlifting when I injured my knee and I took pleasure in learning new skills from different sports, all of which enabled me to do two things: hone into the present moment and relieve stress. Through participating in a variety of activities I discovered what my body was capable of, as well as enabling me to distract myself enough to barricade the mental chatter. Through training and exercise I practised perseverance, focus, and mental stamina.

    The dark side, which doesn't get much time in the limelight, was my abuse with exercise: using it as a form of punishment, desperate to change what I saw in the mirror as I battled with a lack of confidence, or as retribution for the food I ate. While this eventually came to an end, it took many years to overcome via self-awareness and self-discovery, becoming more compassionate with myself. Rediscovering how much I enjoyed physical activity helped break its deployment as a form of self-harm, resulting in a big change in behaviour and attitude.

## HAPPINESS WITHIN

*Enjoy the process; enjoy the journey.*
*Enjoy the discovery of how capable and magnificent your body is.*
*Let go of the punishment you were holding on to and be at peace with how amazing you truly are.*
*Tulshi Varsani*

Once I felt joyful embracing my own strength, appreciating the power my body was capable of exerting, I started to treat it with more loving kindness and pushing past my old barriers: it felt empowering. These jubilant moments enabled me to feel good whilst accomplishing physical challenges and I continue to use training as a form of release (both good and bad). But instead of snapping at people or being angry towards my loved ones, I now remove myself from the situation where possible (particularly avoiding confrontation on things I was unhappy about). This releases my pent-up anger via practising consistent training. This was evident when I found myself using it as a healthy tool instead of a punishment.

I'd always been aware of using exercise to relieve stress, but what changed was my growing awareness as to *why* I was moving my body. I recall being on holiday and seeing an email pop up. As I read the words in black and white, I could feel the blood rise to my face, my heart felt constricted and my breath was becoming short and shallow. I could feel my pent-up anger rising like a volcano about to erupt and although I was able to suppress it enough to respond to the email politely, I hastily navigated my way to the hotel gym. Whilst everyone else was beside the pool, I was in the hotel gym managing my stress and pouring out the emotions I needed to. In that time, I was able to release all the anxiety and frustration that was surging through me and redirected those feelings as energy moving my body. For 90 minutes I took the energy built up via frustration, anger, resentment, and hostility and used it to fuel the workout. I also put on a podcast on forgiveness, which helped me divert my attention from reliving the email. I am certain I would not have been able to overcome that challenge as quickly had I not been able to release it in such a healthy way.

I am now a strength and conditioning performance coach. However, I must admit I was not a sporty person growing up. I enjoyed sports but I was the one who finished amongst the slowest in our year group when competing in the 100-metre sprint during school sports day. I was not the person who committed to a particular sport in school – in fact there were not many options in school. Outside of school I loved being in the water (I adored swimming) and I enjoyed the freedom of movement when dancing with my friends. Once I left for college and moved to university, the exercise stopped for a while, but thankfully this was temporary. I began to take care of my body through training and I realised it was something I could lean on when I was not feeling good about myself, or about life in general. Through my own curiosity I began studying exercise and physiology on the weekends, which eventually led me into the fitness industry, then into the strength and conditioning world. In time, I completed a master's degree in the same field. As my education evolved, I was able to fixate on how people can push themselves mentally as well as physically. That is where my journey changed, as they say:

*If you can't do, teach.*

Unknown

As a child I would line up my bears and dolls pretending I was a teacher in my very own classroom. It is funny to look back that maybe my organisational obsession began here. As an imaginative child, I organised my pupils, created props, and formed lesson plans; later this passion for teaching moulded itself into coaching athletes and corporate clients.

In this chapter I want to expand upon what it means to be flexible, mobile, fitter, stronger, and how this can ensure we are all healthier and happier. Furthermore, this chapter is to uncover how much exercise affects our daily comprehension, our ability to perform and manage success within our lives. Health and wellbeing cannot be discussed without including physical movement: our wellbeing depends on it and our health benefits from it. This chapter, one you may wish to re-read, will focus on the science and for you to uncover your unlimited potential through self-discovery.

The World Health Organisation (WHO) say there is a crisis. Some researchers and media have described sitting as the new smoking but let's get the facts straight. According to the WHO more than 60% of the world's population is not active enough.[1] The evidence clearly indicates activity is essential for personal health and wellbeing. In 2016, more than 1.6 billion adults (eighteen years and older) were overweight. Of these, over 650 million were obese. The number of children under the age of five who were overweight is 41 million.

If obesity is preventable what are the causes of this mass inflation of figures all over the world? Simply put, it is an energy imbalance. We have more access to energy-dense foods. Foods that are higher in fat are more available to us in supermarkets and our working conditions are not as physically stressful. The type of work we do combined with an increase in transportation and urbanisation means an overall increase in sedentary lifestyles. Obesity and being overweight leads directly to having an increased risk of cardiovascular diseases and musculoskeletal disorders, including the increase in cancers.[2] There are far more chances of developing type 2 diabetes, high blood pressure, heart disease, stroke, cancer, sleep apnoea, osteoarthritis, fatty liver disease, kidney disease, and problems with pregnancies.

**Is it worth all these risks?**
It's easy enough to say the reality is, no one is making you eat the food in front of you: it is a decision you are making. Yet sometimes we end up making this decision because we do not feel like we are good enough; we self-harm and depreciate ourselves by eating through our feelings. There are times we reach for unhealthy food because we are unhappy elsewhere in our lives. This disconnect with food means there is a chance of becoming addicted to an unhealthy diet. The food industry is very clever in creating foods that appeal to our taste buds and therefore we continue to buy and eat these to satisfy

those cravings. Although eating mindfully will be a key focus in a separate chapter in this book, we must tackle awareness to this area because understanding cravings will enable you to hear your body's cry for specific nutrients or minerals. Eating well *and* moving more will enable you to make better decisions and when this happens an influx of positives arise:

- You are more alert.
- Your ability to concentrate will increase.
- You will have more energy and (more importantly) you are happier with those you are around.
- You will feel more appreciative and loving towards your body because you are choosing things that benefit you.

But what exactly happens to your body and mind when you exercise and why is this necessary?

**The science of hormones**

When you move your body, your muscles contract and relax; they are stimulated by an activity. Every system in your body focuses its efforts on helping muscles do their work or else your body shuts down. Electrical impulses are sent via your spinal cord from your brain to your nerves so your brain can stimulate muscles to contract. When your brain decides which muscles to contract, feedback mechanisms allow your brain to monitor the movement; this is called 'proprioception'. Proprioception allows your brain to understand where one body part is in relation to others, and in relation to gravity. An important part of the benefits of exercise are the hormones and neurotransmitters (also known as 'catecholamines') which produce different effects on the body.

Your hormone production is regulated by your endocrine system. Hormones are chemicals which control cellular function, and they affect several different cells. Hormones also control physiological reactions such as metabolism, reproductive processes, and moods, to name a few. Each class of hormones has a unique chemical structure, which determines its interactions with receptors. Think in terms of a lock and key principle: a specific key must fit a specific lock to interact with cells and there are thousands of various combinations of keys and locks within your body.

'Norepinephrine' (also called 'noradrenalin') is a catecholamine hormone; it functions as a neurotransmitter in the sympathetic nervous system. Norepinephrine directly affects adrenergic receptors (these constrict blood vessels to increase blood pressure). The direct precursor of norepinephrine is 'dopamine', synthesised indirectly from the essential amino acid 'phenylalanine', which is found in nearly every protein.‡‡ Norepinephrine modifies each organ's state, and it is more conducive to active body movement. The sympathetic effects of norepinephrine increases production of tears, increases the amount of blood pumped into the heart, aids the pancreas by increasing the release of glucagon (and producing glucose by the liver), and helps glucose increase its uptake to skeletal muscles, to name but a few. When activated, noradrenergic neurons in the brain form a neurotransmitter system which manifests as alertness, arousal, and readiness for action.

'Epinephrine' (known as adrenaline) releases in response to stress and is another catecholamine hormone. Unlike norepinephrine, epinephrine does not have its own receptors. It mainly acts as a hormone. It increases blood sugar levels and heart rate, relaxes the airways to improve breathing, and provides your body with extra energy when you are stressed, in shock, or are afraid. Lower levels of epinephrine (either as a neurotransmitter or hormone) contribute greatly to physical and mental conditions including anxiety, depression, migraines, and sleep disorders. Higher levels cause an increase in blood pressure and heart palpitations.

**Exercise and cognitive functioning**

When you attempt to move your body, your brain initially recognises this as *stress*. As your heart pressure increases and neurotransmitters and hormones are released, your

---

‡‡ Phenylalanine is an amino acid found in mother's milk and a number of foods, including meat, poultry, fish, cottage cheese, lentils, peanuts and sesame seeds.

cognitive function deciphers between whether this is a life-or-death scenario: also known as 'fight-or-flight'. A protein called BDNF (brain-derived neurotrophic factor) acts as a reset switch, while endorphins are also released by your brain. This protein minimises physical pain and discomfort, replacing it with a feeling of euphoria.

Growing evidence indicates both fasting and exercise trigger genes and growth factors that recycle and rejuvenate your brain and muscle tissues. Some studies show dietary restriction stimulates the production of new neurons, increasing the brain's ability to resist ageing and restore function to the brain following injury. This appears to result in a stress response at a cellular level, stimulating neuronal plasticity[§§] and the productions of certain proteins, such as BDNF.[3,4] This protein is active in both muscles *and* your brain: it is this cross connection that appears to be a major factor in explaining why a physical workout can benefit the impact of brain tissues.

The BDNF protein is thought to be an essential ingredient in combatting anxiety. Scientists think this may be due to the brain learning how to work around the fear and create positive memories.[5] Furthermore, higher levels of this protein increase levels of serotonin. This in turn gives you a sense of calmness and increases your sense of safety. This is probably the reason why when you are feeling anxious or frustrated, taking yourself out for a run or doing some sort of physical activity allows your brain to think of solutions and decrease the levels of anxiety you may have previously experienced. Lower levels of anxiety create a much calmer state, which often provides the best opportunity for ideas or creative solutions.

---

[§§] Neuronal plasticity, also known as neuroplasticity, refers to the ability of the brain to change and adapt in response to an experience. This can take many forms, such as the formation of new connections between neurons, or the creation of new neurons (a process called 'neurogenesis'). Neuronal plasticity is thought to be an important mechanism underlying learning and memory, as well as the brain's ability to recover from injury. It is also believed to play a role in the development of certain mental health conditions such as depression and anxiety.

Where can we get more of these feel-good proteins? Well, scientists have been able to decipher that exercise increases their production and adjusts them to the optimal levels we need. Furthermore, BDNF has contributed to the evolution of the human brain. Although it is not the primary or sole factor, BDNF can modify our DNA by developing our higher cognitive functions, such as language and abstract thought. Carl Cotman, a neuroscientist, ran an experiment with rats where he monitored differences in BDNF productions between various exercise routines. After only two weeks, the rats who exercised daily produced this protein more rapidly than the rats who exercised on alternating days (150% of baseline versus 124% baseline). However, after a month, there was no difference in production of BDNF between those who exercised daily and those who exercised every other day. The study also observed the protein returned to baseline after only two weeks of not exercising. This was the same conclusion for both groups. The levels then rose again after two days of exercising: 139% for daily exercisers and 129% for alternating day exercisers.[6]

Another great find from the research was that older rats were just as proficient as the young rats in producing BDNF. BDNF is also active in the hippocampus, an area which is tasked with encoding new memories and learning new information. Lacking BDNF here leads to dementia, depression, and memory loss. A lack of BDNF paralyses the hippocampus by weakening the synaptic strength. What does that mean? Well, if those neuron signals are a lot weaker, the hippocampus neurons become more vulnerable to stressors and atrophy. Consequently, blocking production of BDNF in the hippocampus reduces long-term memory persistence. BDNF production in the hippocampus reverses the impairment of long-term memory.[7] Therefore, if exercising or taking up sport increases the levels of BDNF production – which in turn lowers stress, symptoms of mental illnesses, as well as increasing your ability to strengthen your long-term memory – then exercise essentially allows your brain to learn more effectively.

The amygdala respond to different sensory modalities such as sight, sound, and touch.[***] It influences and uses information to determine emotional significance of a given stimuli. The amygdala sends the outputs to other brain regions. The hippocampus plays a role in processing sensory information and regulating emotions.[†††] Emotional tension can initiate a stress response via the sympathetic nervous system, which culminates in adrenaline and cortisol racing through your entire body. The logical portion of your brain will attempt to restrain the emotional part of your brain by triggering your parasympathetic nervous system to signal the body to relax.

Yoga can train the body to hold a specific posture, and maintaining balance engages the logical part of your brain. The result is that you are focused and logical. When you train your mind to raise the parasympathetic signal you train your mind to keep perceived stress under control. This is why the overall culture of yoga emphasises it being a way of life – not just a training or workout session. Yoga provides tools that are conducive to your daily life; particularly useful for when difficult times arise and cause physiological stress response.

Chemicals such as serotonin and dopamine are released instigating the process of restoration and healing through your parasympathetic nervous system:[‡‡‡] as your blood pressure is lowered it is directed towards the endocrine glands, digestive organs, and lymphatic circulation. Your heart rate is therefore lowered, and nutrients are absorbed more easily as improved circulation releases toxins from the body. Exercise enhances your cognitive function, thus allowing the body to

---

[***] The amygdala is located in the medial prefrontal cortex part of the brain. It's small and shaped like an almond.

[†††] The hippocampus is found in the medial temporal lobe. Shaped like a seahorse, it is located deep in the brain and is involved in the formation and consolidation of long-term memories.

[‡‡‡] Serotonin is a neurotransmitter involved in regulating mood, anxiety, and aggression. It is also involved in controlling sleep, appetite, and other behaviours. Dopamine is a neurotransmitter that is involved in brain function including movement, reward, motivation, and pleasure. It is also believed to be connected to motivation, cognition, and mood regulation.

be more efficient in regulating its hormones which correlates to my following point on exercise and productivity.

**Exercise and productivity**
Even when you have employed various tools at your disposal – you have written a schedule, adjusted your workflow, you've even created a system of productivity – there will still be one missing component that would increase your productivity by 21%. The magic formula? It comes directly from exercising.

Two hundred employees at three organisations were a part of a study conducted by Coulson et al.[6] It is difficult to measure productivity as such, however Coulson's study gave employees a chance to self-evaluate their own performance. Employees evaluated themselves on days which included and excluded exercise. Participants felt on the days they partook in exercise their evaluation scores improved significantly. Their scores were as follows:

- 21% higher for concentration on work.
- 22% finished their work on time.
- 25% higher for working without unscheduled breaks.
- 41% felt more motivated to work.

A study by Pronk et al. found 30 minutes of exercise significantly improved impacted employee work performance and rate of productivity.[7] Another study by Del Giorno et al. showed an increase in attention, memory, and problem-solving after vigorous cycling, effects which continued for 20 minutes (at which point the researchers stopped tracking). The group that cycled at a slower pace were unaffected. Numerous other studies have found increased productivity and happiness on any given day as a result of long-term investment in regular exercise.[8] There is a short-term boost to your mood and over time you are able to sharpen your cognition. The first 20 minutes of moving around (if someone has been extremely sedentary) can provide the most health benefits such as prolonged life and reducing risks of diseases. Other interesting results from this study were:

- 72% improved their time management on exercise versus non-exercise days.
- 79% improved their mental and interpersonal performance on exercise days.

Whether you feel like it or not, take a moment to move your body, knowing your body will respond when you move it. You can make the initial decision to get on a bike, go for a swim, or – better yet – a walk outdoors; all of which are helpful in improving your body's responses to how you feel. Researchers at Michigan University gave two groups a brief memory test. One group took a walk around the arboretum, the other group took a walk down a city street. When both groups returned, those who had walked amongst the trees performed almost 20% better in the memory test in comparison to their initial assessment result.[9]

Does mood and energy improve your productivity? Possibly. The University of Glasgow found an increase in productivity and its association with a longer workout in the morning. Any physical activity, including mild to low intensity exercise such as walking, yoga, golf, or dancing will prove significant to your productivity.[10] Do not be deceived into thinking one training session will make a significant difference to your mind and body; adopting *consistent* effort will gradually progress your strength and fitness, and may well increase your levels of production – and, consequently, success. If we see levels of productivity and success linking with one another, we must also be willing to consider and understand how valuable rest and recovery is. Many of us, myself included, may have believed the hype growing up regarding 'sleep less, do more'. It was the influence of many successful people who were determined to spread to notion of persevering through lack of sleep, as rest was considered meaningless and a waste of time. For me, my productivity is highest in the mornings, which means I am less likely to stay up late the night before. In chapter nine I will delve more into the relationship between sleep and wellbeing.

### Exercise, relationships, and happiness

My personal relationship with exercise gave me two – quite different – experiences. On the one hand I would pound the road for hours at a time and rejoice in the moments where I could be in complete solitude, deliberate on my thoughts, and manage my own pace. The other version was when I would seek support from my friends, finding their encouragement enabled me to put in more effort when training. Both methods increased my strength and gave me consistent motivation; however, when training with someone whom I connected with, it not only enhanced my workouts, it also increased my joy and enthusiasm. I tended to enjoy those sessions far more than if I had participated alone.

As we get older, making friends can become difficult. Friendships tend to form in school and university but as we navigate through our own path, find new hobbies, and focus on our career, some friendships fade, while others flourish. Careers tend to lead us into new areas and similar schedules; therefore, if you're lucky, it's natural to bond with those you work with. We find our time and energy becomes an extremely valued type of currency, and so we must choose who deserves it most. We understand that although technology connects us to others around the world, we can also create a more insular lifestyle. This is impacting our long-term mental health and we have figures that tell us that millennials are the most isolated generation:

- 30% state they often feel lonely.
- 25% of millennials are more likely to report they have no acquaintances.
- 22% say they have no friends.
- 27% say they have no close friends.
- 30% claim they have no best friends.

One in five members from Generation X claim to feel lonely, and approximately three out of ten claim they find it difficult to make friends. Over a quarter (26%) claim to not have any hobbies or interests that facilitate friendships.[11] So how do people make friends or form relationships? Is it within high school, university, our jobs, our neighbourhood, or within a spiritual community? All is not lost: the good news is that 33% of people meet their friends through sport or by participating in fitness activities.[11] People can work together towards a common goal during training, this is noticeable in team-based types of activities, which brings individuals together, particularly during competitions. Training will also cultivate your personal relationship with your own self-esteem and your body.

*In order to love others, you must first love yourself.*
Unknown

When participating in training you will start to appreciate your capabilities, your strengths, and you will begin to nurture your accomplishments. In turn, many of your qualities will enhance your health and wellbeing, and you naturally attract aspects you need in order to take care of yourself. As we age, it is inevitable that there will be a natural decline in our physical and cognitive functions. As noted above, millennials are becoming more isolated and it is common that as we age our social networks reduce too.[12]

Cohen and Wills studied positive social relationships and health outcomes, concluding that there are positive trends in promoting healthy behaviours centred on social relationships and these behaviours remained positive despite any stress the individuals may be experiencing at the time.[12] Those who enhance their social relationships not only improve their psychological wellbeing but their physical health too. There is an increased sense of belonging as well as enhancing immune function and reducing the risk of heart attacks.[13] Physical activity can help regain feelings of purpose and feeling needed, particularly within a collective group activity. A life-fulfilled study found participants aged sixty or older (in the retirement transition period) spent their time participating in leisurely activities.[14] Thirty-nine papers met the inclusion criteria[§§§] and have been synthesised to suggest that as individuals transition to older age there is a challenge regarding people's sense of self and their role in life. In another study, researchers examined 2,965 older adults during the years of 2006–2010 to study the link between social relationships and health. They demonstrated that leisure activities mediate the link between social relationships and health because there was greater involvement within leisure activities.[12]

Children, specifically those in middle childhood, are in a crucial stage for developing healthy friendships, learning to think independently, and dealing with peer pressure.[15] Adolescents who scored highest in leadership skills were physically active on a weekly basis (≥ 20 min/day) and also showed higher scores in increasing characteristics such as empathy. Those who were more physically active (≥ 30 min/day), including participating in team sports, were associated with higher leadership empathy scores.[16]

More importantly, these healthier behaviours allow adolescents to care not only about their own health but about the health of others. Participating in a team sport increases individuals' communication and these interactions can be seen on many other levels. They include connections with the coaching team such as managers, strength and conditioning coaches, physical therapists, referees, and organisers, as well as connecting with other players on the team. It allows individuals to be a part of a group, and this is where the leadership opportunities can thrive. Boosts in self-esteem when playing a sport or participating in exercise nurtures confidence. It also allows children and adults to stand up for themselves and others.

The benefits of creating such social connections permit building a foundation of personal fulfilment and happiness.

---

[§§§] These are the requirements or characteristics that must be met in order for a person or thing to be included in a study, programme, or process. It is often used to ensure that a study or evaluation is representative and the results are generalisable to a larger population. Some factors include age, gender, health status, etc.

Sport allows people to have a sense of belonging and develop feelings of self-worth. It provides individuals with a sense of security in their own decisions, as well as drawing comfort in knowing they can seek assistance from others. These bonds forge a connection that when individuals suffer, experience hardships, or challenges, they are more likely to call upon others who have gone through similar encounters, or those they share common goals and interests with. A study by Seligman and Diener took a sample of 222 undergraduates who were screened for high happiness using multiple confirming assessment filters. The very happy people were highly social and had strong romantic and other social relationships than less happy groups. Very happy people also have a functioning emotion system which enables them to react appropriately to life's events.[17] Building a social network that has a general attitude of positivity will rub off on you: the company you keep will influence your behaviours and moods.

Successful marriages can be a great example of partners supporting one another, enhancing their individual levels of happiness as well as happiness within the partnership. Gyms, the finish lines of marathons, and sports events have all provided perfect locations for marriage proposals. I personally know of two couples who proposed at the very end of their partner's competition. I also know many more couples who have met in their local gyms. There is no shying away from the fact that exercise can be a method of strengthening relationships, no matter the type. Dr Christina Hibbert claims couples who exercise together increase their time spent together, tend to have healthier connections in communication, and are modelling exercise for their younger siblings and or children.[18, 19]

As with everything, when taking part in something new it often begins with good intention, and high levels of motivation and enthusiasm. However, it takes on average 66 days to form a new habit. It takes time for something new to become routine, it also takes time to see the rewards of those consistent behaviours. For us to gain the reward we must be patient and preserve consistency within those efforts. As we know, we will not see benefits straightaway; this is where persistence is key. Seek out another person who can mirror your level of competency: this will allow you both to learn something new and enjoy participating in an activity. This connection will enhance your commitment to your chosen activity because you are now accountable to someone else other than yourself.

Having a relationship with someone you can enjoy training with will enhance your relationship with each other. You will be able to enjoy the present moment by participating in physical activity as well as forging a relationship with your personal health. Training with your partner or within a sports team will bring about a sense of togetherness and unity, particularly when facing challenges as a team. In turn, this leads to more excitement and happiness surrounding your training, which strengthens your desire to exercise. A study where mothers and daughters took part in a twelve-week programme agreed their relationships improved significantly because of the physical activities they took part in.[18]

My own training journey gave me a chance to develop my personal goals; my dedication and relationships also flourished when training with others. Both gave me huge benefits, yet one was not better than the other. For me, they both served their goals enhancing my personal and physical development. I invite you to experiment with this companion-based type of training. Start by participating in various sports. Begin with doing what you enjoy and discover what suits your style of training. You may be as I used to be: someone who craved solitude and independence, who later discovered that support and encouragement from others was another way to enjoy training. Within that time spent training with others I attracted and gained exactly what I needed for my mental and physical wellbeing.

## TIME TO CONSIDER

1) **Organise an evening with friends based on an activity of your choice.**
   It could be yoga, tennis, rugby – anything that involves exercising with other people. However, ensure you extend

your circle to include those you may not usually hang around with. The purpose is to find *new* relationships based on the activity, not to base the activity on your current friends.

2) **Go beyond your current friendship circle.**
Invite others via posting on your social media, on the work notice board, or within your work channels.

This can be extremely useful if you have moved to a new area: it is a great way to form new connections outside of work and enables you to have purpose beyond your work life.

3) **Exercise with friends or romantic partners to enhance your relationship.**
If you choose to enhance your current friendship or relationship with a partner, introduce something where you are both able to connect and then enhance the ways you communicate with each other. Perhaps go rock climbing, hiking, play netball, or head to the trampoline park. Treat it as an alternative to your traditional date night!

4) **Find a dance group and encourage your girlfriends to join.**
This is a sure-fire way to build up confidence and bond with one another. No one is in competition with one another: you can just have fun and move! It's the perfect opportunity to prove you don't take yourself too seriously.

Those who are more successful are the ones who have found what type of healthy lifestyle works for them. Many successful people use exercise as a habit; they match what works for them daily. Whether it is on the treadmill, cycling, dancing, ballet, or running, the key to building this habit is to forget the end goal.

Take for example dieting or healthy eating: there is no end goal, *not really*. You start to eat reasonably healthy because of what you are choosing for yourself: the more you appreciate yourself, the better you will treat your body. When you achieve your goal weight, should you revert to your old habits, all that previous work you put in will be reversed. Therefore, those old habits no longer serve you. Your new habits will need to continue from here on in to sustain your new look or physique and support your current energy levels. However, once you have figured out your personal process and schedule, you will be more likely to enjoy life, you will be less likely to cut corners and allow for such accommodations within your lifestyle. You will no longer refuse meals out with friends or dismiss small indulgences because you know, overall, your health and wellbeing are consistent.

My hope is that you will grow self-love and compassion; you will be more inclined to be kinder to yourself with what you eat; your body will respond and reward you by increasing your energy levels, focus, attention, productivity, and success – not only in your health but in many other areas of your life. Physical exercise alone is not enough. Scientists and nutritionists claim the pathway to fitness lies within a holistic lifestyle. We must understand exercise alone will not make you a healthier person as you will need to also adjust the way you eat. Key components of physical, mental, and nutritional health combined ensure your mind and body function equally well.

## CHAPTER EIGHT: CONSCIOUS EATING

*Life will throw you curve balls. There are a lot of uncontrollable situations but the one thing you can control is what you put into your body.*
Tulshi Varsani

I leant over the sink and thought to myself, *This is the only time I'll do this. I will not let myself eat so badly again.* I washed my mouth and left the bathroom. I had thrown up. Back then I used food to mask my feelings. I did not address what the real issue was, I simply acknowledged I was unhappy, and this was an avenue I used to handle it. At the time, I did not recognise this as self-harm; I identified it as the one thing I felt I had control over, and I did not think of it as a big deal. Although it happened more than once, I always saw it as a one-off. I justified my behaviour and made excuses due to there being a lack of frequency and regularity. In fact, I didn't know then, the excuses I made up to justify my behaviour.

I also ensured it was kept secret. No one knew. My best friend at the time suffered with anorexia. I was still in high school and felt it was not something I could speak to anyone about. As a result, I dismissed it because I was unable to see through my own smoky mirrors. It took me an extremely long time to discover food was a mask, an unhealthy habit that clouded my judgement and enabled me to suppress any underlying feelings I may have been experiencing. Feelings included being lost, unhappy, unloved ... I did not know why or how to assess those feelings, nor did I know how to resolve them.

As mentioned in earlier chapters, my childhood was a happy one, yet it did not relate to how I felt in this world during that time in my life. This was a destructive path I went down. I knew, even then, it felt wrong and yet I continued to abuse my body with every unhealthy decision I had made. I knew I did not want to be influenced by such a negative pattern of behaviour, yet I simply didn't know where to start. Somehow, as this pattern continued into my early twenties, the awareness came: I recognised what I was doing and I forced myself to do better, but this took years to overcome. Having this damaging obsession with food was a way to distract myself from how I really felt.

Even to this day, not many people know what happened, as I refused to discuss it with anyone, maybe if I didn't revisit it, I could erase that memory. I admit, during writing this book I contemplated whether I should omit this chapter. I went back and forth on whether it was a good idea, but I soon realised I could not discuss physical wellbeing without including food and mindfulness. My initial fear was that putting my thoughts and experiences on paper regarding this failure, or flaw, where everyone could see and read it, made it all too real. Nonetheless, I realised if I went through this and told no one, it wouldn't be useful. That there would certainly be others in this world who may have been through similar thoughts and/or experiences. There may also be someone who thinks they need to hide or continue this behaviour alone. This made the decision to keep this chapter in easier because I needed to showcase how it made me feel, thereby opening doors for others to overcome their circumstances. To know, you are not alone. Should you find this chapter somewhat upsetting, particularly for those who have ever experienced disordered eating or an eating disorder. Please seek help and support if you find you are experiencing a disordered eating response to the following content.

Although I can't recall how this obsession and destructive habit formed, I recognised at some point, perhaps in my adolescence I would eat when I was not hungry and then continued to eat. I would eat in private and hide things from my family. When you begin to drown your emotions with food, it can be quickly followed by shame and accompanied with feelings of guilt. If you or someone you know is experiencing symptoms of this, please seek advice from a health professional or your GP. Tell a friend how you are feeling and talk to someone who can help. Just because I didn't doesn't mean you cannot; there are many avenues you can seek support from. I also want to add that I am not a professional when it comes to disordered eating or eating disorders. Like many of the passages in this book, what follows is based on my own experience. I often refer *how to avoid overeating* because that was the tool I employed to cope with a troubling time in my life. However, mindful or conscious eating can also help those who are obsessed with healthy eating such as 'orthorexia'.[****]

Everyone's experiences and causes differ. If, like me, you've become aware of binge eating, you may ask yourself whether it has stemmed from boredom; is it habitual or associated with the people you are surrounding yourself with? It may even be because you are experiencing depression: scientists are not sure whether depression causes binge eating or vice versa. For me, I did not realise the state of mind I was in until it overtook my physical actions.

Binge eating is the most common way of dealing with negative emotions.[1] Rational, functioning adults can totally lose control of their impulses and there are occasions where random indulgences become a real problem. Things such as powerlessness, secrecy, shame, and social isolation can lead to individuals binging. Binge eating is common for those who have a family history of eating disorders or for people who have experienced trauma or stress. It is also common for individuals who have certain mental health conditions such as

---

[****] This is a term for an unhealthy obsession with 'clean' eating. People become fixated on the quality, purity, and quantity of food they eat; to the point that it interferes with their daily life and wellbeing. This obsession can lead to malnutrition, social isolation, and other negative physical and mental health consequences.

depression, anxiety, or substance abuse disorders. There are the three major contributing factors.

**Psychological**
Anxiety, stress, and/or depression are the underlying reasons why people feel the need to numb their pain or hide their feelings. Low esteem, body disfunction, and poor impulse control can all trigger a binge.

**Chemical**
A dopamine hit kicks in when a person overindulges and it feels good, but only temporarily. Eating sugar and/or processed foods, and drinking alcohol can all become a physical addiction. A person may begin to crave the consumables that provide a neurological chemical release, which can in turn lead to compulsive behaviours such as binge eating.

**Sociocultural**
Self-confidence and feeling pressure from culture can drive individuals to binge. Society places great emphasis on external beauty, youthfulness, and size. This has formed unhealthy behaviours as aesthetic expectations are increased amongst younger women and men. There are many theories as to why eating disorders are more prevalent in females than males: author and professor Kelly Klump believes one of the main reasons includes the increasing cultural and psychological pressure girls and women face.[2]

**Mindful eating**
The key thing when looking at food and dealing with emotions is to be mindful of both these things. If you choose to eat or choose not to eat, delve deeper into what you are feeling during that time. This is where you can begin to understand your emotions. We so often let our emotions control our food intake, but this is where our awareness needs to be present. First, we need to tackle what is already going on in our heads and be mindful *before* implementing change. I know a friend who was conscious to the fact he was not eating after a

breakup; he certainly wasn't aware that he was playing the victim role because he proclaimed the benefits of losing weight! This is a classic example of using our emotions to manipulate our food habits.

Many people think they haven't an issue around food because their narrative is, *I'm no longer abusing myself if I do not overeat.* However, self-harm is just as prominent if you have ever gone days or weeks without properly eating, occurrences maybe dependent on circumstances, i.e. Work is busy, my projects or kids are my priority, my partner broke up with me. It is not the way to lose weight; it is not healthy; nor will it ever be beneficial towards your productivity and consequent successes. Your health and wellbeing are and should always be your priority. Your awareness is what brings you to this point. Riding the waves in your emotional wellbeing means you are more likely to take hold of chaotic situations within your life. This also enables you to be conscious and more capable of dealing with a variety of stressful situations.

Let me be clear, this chapter distinguishes between serious cases – where you acknowledge and seek professional help and cases where you need to raise awareness for your wellness and wellbeing. I want to use my own experiences to help those who have disordered eating traits, which include binging, restless eating, including consuming out of boredom.

Eating without consciousness can stem from something as habitual as picking up your phone. We often use our phones while eating; this is an unhealthy habit which often occurs when we are left alone or bored with the present moment. That can even include when you are around your friends. Perhaps you are looking for more engagement or attention; whatever it may be, you are taken away from the present moment and this distraction is to engage in another one that can feel more satisfying.

Some people create an unhealthy habit of always eating when watching television, or even eating at their desks at work. This harmful behaviour can often be prompted by a personal or professional influence, such as a deadline at work. Maybe you want to be seen as a keen worker or someone who is passionate about their role compared to others in your team. However, each one of these examples have a common theme: eating without any awareness, which creates unhealthy patterns. By being present and eating in a way that allows us to taste the food, we can enjoy our meals and listen to our body, particularly when it tells us that we are full. Eating without consciousness of our actions tends to lead us down a slippery slope, where we discover we are in a state of mindless eating. This is akin to those occasions when you are watching a movie and you reach into the bottom of the bag of snacks, only to find it is already empty. Eating while doing something else (such as watching TV or using your phone) causes you to mindlessly consume more food than you need.

First, let's navigate through raising awareness. Are there times you have made allowances for consuming foods you may not have usually? A well-known study demonstrated how psychologically healthy eating is trumped by the irrational 'mind in the stomach'. Participants in this study were fooled into eating from a bottomless bowl of soup (it was pressure-fed through the bottom of the table as they ate).[3] The participants were led to believe they were simply eating slower than normal; in fact it was their mind that was convincing them of this thought. This caused them to mindlessly swallow 73% more soup than those who ate from the unmodified 22 oz bowls. Similar convictions have been found when drinking. Participants drank 27% more if they were drinking from a short and wide tumbler than those who drank from a tall, slender tumbler. The cause? A simple deception of the horizontal-vertical illusion.

Being mindful whilst you eat develops awareness of internal hunger and satiety cues that allow you to make conscious food choices. Paying attention to those cues (emotionally and physically) while eating will mean you get to eat what you want and enjoy the taste of it all. Have you ever experienced being present with what you are eating without thinking of where you must be next or scrolling through social media? Have you ever taken your time to chew and fulfil those joyous emotions when eating good food, satisfying your taste buds, and enjoying the sometimes-labour-intensive food you have taken time to make, only to find you have consumed it within ten minutes? When you take time to eat the food you want, you enjoy it, and you are satisfying the intent and the craving. You are not depriving yourself of foods that taste good, neither are you restricting yourself from all unhealthy foods. Knowing what food does to your body and paying attention to what you feel when you eat will soon allow you to be aware of eating for hunger versus eating out of boredom or using food to push down certain emotions you no longer want to feel from real-life scenarios or events.

Your body is very clever: it signals your various needs and wants all day. The problem is we rarely take the time to listen. Take, for example, a signal for thirst. You will crave something that can quench your thirst as soon as your body detects minor symptoms of dehydration. Instead of reaching for water (which would be the obvious solution) many people reach for a snack or sugary drink. Sugar cravings are usually a by-product of hormonal imbalance, stress, or fatigue. This lack of awareness not only creates extra calories, but it also increases swelling, sensitivity, soreness, infection, and pain within your body. Inflammation is a possible side effect you may not have even noticed, because much of this is experienced inside your body without your knowledge.

Discovering and raising your awareness of the difference between thirst and hunger is a basic but simple strategy that can be implemented immediately. Taking on this one habit will address and most likely illuminate when you are eating out of boredom. This is a common but useful reminder: try drinking water 20–30 minutes before you plan to eat. As well as satisfying your thirst, water helps flush out toxins from your body and aids your digestive system. This is also helpful when you sense what you perceive to be hunger. After drinking water, you may find your food craving has dissipated. Of course, if you find you are still hungry after drinking water, this is now your body confirming to you it's needs. This is also a reminder for those who are all consumed and too busy, failing to eat regularly or ignoring hunger cues. Attempt to bring awareness to how much energy you have during your day and begin to prioritise nutrient-dense foods. Some clients, who own their own businesses and are highly successful, have tendencies to reach for easy, fast foods to satisfy their early satiety. Some consume too little and tend to gain excess weight due to irregularity of their meals.

Find foods that satisfy your hunger and provide nutrients that will energise you throughout your day. This is not about restricting foods you enjoy eating; it is more about taking note of how much you need to eat. When eating out, you aren't given appropriate portions, when eating alone, you may consume more than required but once you begin to restrict foods within your diet, your body and brain will begin to crave that type of food more than usual, which can often trigger a binge. Restriction can be harmful if you are unaware of your actions, thoughts, and emotions.

Where possible, you should always eat when you want to and not when you are supposed to. This is known as intuitive eating. When it comes to weight loss, it is not clear that intuitive eating is more effective than calorie restriction, but observational studies found people who eat intuitively have a lower BMI (body mass index) than those who do not.[4] Eating intuitively may reduce the number of times a person binge eats; it is also associated with positive body image and high self-esteem. Of course, there are times when intuitive eating is not always practical. Those who work in a shift pattern or need to accommodate for family mealtimes will find that meal timing is based around events or occasions beyond your control.

**Healthy gut equals healthy mind**
Healthy eating patterns are associated with positive health outcomes, as reflected by the United Kingdom's Government dietary guidelines.[5, 6] We know eating healthily reduces our risks of cardiovascular diseases, diabetes, and certain types of cancers. Yet so many well-informed people binge eat, even if they are already aware of the evidence that supports eating healthily. The Mental Health Foundation notes eating well is important for mental health, as it plays a vital role in the development, management, and prevention of several specific conditions, including schizophrenia, depression,

attention deficit hyperactivity disorder, and Alzheimer's disease.[7] Diet alone will not be able to control these conditions, but diet may play a significant role alongside other treatments when attempting to manage those diseases.

I recall a period when I was addicted to sugar. I am sure we have all been there at some point during our lives, unless you are the type who does not have a sweet tooth! What I had noticed was eventually my body began to reject this overwhelming amount of sugar I was ingesting because I failed to consider how much I was consuming. I began to experience horrid headaches, which sometimes turned into debilitating migraines. I noticed my teeth becoming extremely sensitive, my skin was not happy with this excess either and I would break out in rashes and spots. I even had moments where I began to feel more bloated, and then I noticed excess weight was piling around my stomach. This was when I was in my early twenties: all because of sugar!

The result of finding inner happiness means it radiates outwards through our pores. Conversely, feeling stressed, depressed, or anxious results in a whole range of physical ailments. When individuals experience stress, problems such as tension headaches arise. There is higher risk of heartburn as your stomach releases more acid than normal. You increase the risk of heart attacks because of the way you breathe. Your blood vessels tighten which leads to your blood pressure increasing. Stress can weaken the immune system, which makes you more susceptible to infections. During stress your liver also releases more sugar into your bloodstream; over time that can put you at risk for type 2 diabetes.

As well as the effects of stress on the body, the foods we consume can have a direct impact on the way your body digests and removes toxins from your body. There is evidence that dietary choices can help manage the symptoms of various diseases. Research also indicates you can safeguard a healthy brain into your old age if you add foods that enrich it. Here are a few examples:[8]

**Blueberries**
Found to contain protective components for your brain, they reduce the effects of age-related conditions such as Alzheimer's (placing genetic predisposition aside). This nutrient-rich food reduces oxidative stress, demonstrating improvements in learning capacity and motor skills in ageing rates.

**Nuts and seeds**
Have properties which correspond with less cognitive decline because they contain higher levels of vitamin E.

**Avocados**
Give the system monosaturated fats, contributing to healthy blood flow; this in turn affects the brain and lowers blood pressure.

**Dark chocolate**
Boosts the production of endorphins which encourages a shift in mood. Also provides other antioxidant properties because it contains natural stimulants such as caffeine.

**Turmeric**
A powerful anti-inflammatory nutrient that can support the reduction in inflammation related to arthritis, diabetes, and other diseases.

These examples inform us that we need to nurture our body and brain in order for us to function in the best way we can; not only for our daily routine but to enhance our levels of creativity and cognitive capabilities. The Risk Index for Depression (RID), developed by Dr Joanna Dipnall, revealed individuals are prone to depression if their diet is poor, their lifestyle is erratic, and if they do not exercise.[9] Dr Dipnall also asserts that a diet rich in fibre is the key to a healthy mind.

The relationship between obesity and mental health problems is extremely complex. Results in 2010 produced a systematic review that found a two-way association between depression and obesity. The findings concluded that those who were obese had a 55% increased risk for developing depression over time, while people experiencing depression had a 58% risk of becoming obese. According to a study in *Annals of Neurology,* men who follow a Mediterranean style of eating are less likely to suffer from strokes, depression, and declining mental function in older age.[10] Studies pooled findings from 22 different areas, including 11 on Mediterranean eating and stroke risk.[11]

**Eating for performance**
Being happy and healthy involves conscious eating. Navigating through conscious eating and facing the harsh reality between emotions and attachment to food is important. Mindlessly overeating, or unconsciously undereating, occurs when there is a disassociation between eating and your emotions. The same principle applies if you only eat for energy or fuel. There are countless athletes and individuals who develop an unhealthy relationship with food and they too fluctuate with their weight depending on the competition and timeline for their chosen sport.

Take weightlifting and boxing as two examples. These sports involve many restrictive diets to ensure the individuals are primed for their specific weight category. Unfortunately, some athletes have never received formal guidance on how to fuel their body for performance, let alone attempted to decipher all the random advice from so-called experts regarding food online. Even for athletes such as rowers and swimmers, there is a misconception that individuals who are in a high energy demanding profession may eat whatever they like, yet this is the biggest faux pas.

Choices must be nutrient-dense as well as tailoring macronutrients and micronutrients for the individual's personal sports and body composition. We have not even begun to discuss hormonal fluctuations such as oestrogen and progesterone during female menstruation.†††† Nutrition is a complex science: a person's metabolism, weight, age, gender, and body composition all add up to the personal criteria. Individual nutrition plans are key to gain the most successful performance outcome. There are many key components when assessing nutrients for an athlete which influence the rigid structure created to match their weekly training schedules as well as leading up to competitions. The specifics on how to balance this ensures insulin levels remain balanced and therefore neither crash nor peak too early before finishing a competition.

It is key to seek professional advice before pushing your body through various events: the goal is to advance towards your competition in the healthiest way. This means producing the best possible outcome for *your body* in order to perform at your peak. Females are also a different paradigm when it comes to nutrition as there may naturally be deficiencies in certain micronutrients such as calcium, vitamin D, and iron, to name a few examples. The main consideration to note is whether you are a fit individual or someone who simply wants to perform within their business or job: you will need to find what works for you and make changes that are manageable and sustainable in your daily life.

## TIME TO CONSIDER

1) **Recognition**
Write down your feelings about your relationship with food. Are you someone who justifies eating certain food or drinks?

A common way to address this is to simply observe your feelings before you eat. Throughout the day this will hone into your current state of mind and what you reach for as a consequence.

---

††††RED-S (Relative Energy Deficiency in Sport) highlights over-training and under-fueling, affecting both men and women. Symptoms include an erratic menstrual cycle, weight loss, tiredness, injury, low mood, and poor performance.[12]

2) **Address**
    - Do you feel guilty when consuming particular foods?
    - When is this most likely and why do you feel guilty?
    - Have you deprived yourself of food when feeling emotional?

    Emotions and feelings include anger, upset, fear, sadness, unhappiness, fatigue; to name a few. Try and expand your repertoire of feelings and dig deeper if these are repetitive.

3) **Habits**
    This is a good time to address *how* you eat:
    - Are you able to quantify your current habits?
    - What habits are you currently engaging in that are associated with food?
    - Do you unconsciously or mindlessly eat whilst watching television or while sitting at your desk at work?
    - Do you use food to fuel your body for energy, or do you fit it in when you can around your work/family duties?

4) **Seek support**
    If any of these answers make you aware you are unable to control your feelings and emotions around food, you may want to consider seeking professional support. There are two avenues depending on what it is you need. Either you seek a dietician (a qualified health professional that can assess, diagnose, and treat dietary and nutritional problems – they must be registered to practise within their field) or a nutritionist (qualified to provide information about food and healthy eating – their title is not protected by law). There are also charities and support online: find something that suits you and your location.

Whether you are someone who has noticed changes in a friend's behaviour associated with food, or you have experienced this uncertainty yourself, know you are not alone. With conscious awareness and clear guidance you will be able to manage ways in which you can create healthier habits for your mind and body. Using these tools, you will find you are rewarded via boosts in energy, productivity, attention, and focus. This path is not linear: there are times that will test your mental resilience, patience, and attitude. Celebrations and occasions may derail your progress but remember the 80/20 rule when that happens. Eat well for 80% of the time and use the remaining 20% to let yourself enjoy the foods you normally wouldn't.

# CHAPTER NINE: YOU SNOOZE, YOU WIN

*If you get tired, learn to rest, not to quit*
Banksy

If you asked me what the one solution is to regulate weight, increase cognition, and give you a feeling of health, wellness, and vitality, my answer would be sleep. Sleeping is a basic human need, and it is the third most valuable, underutilised resource we need for our body, but so regularly mismanaged. (The other two-thirds, if you were wondering, include physical activity and nutrition). These three pillars form the foundation of your lifestyle pyramid: everything after these three components will be higher up the pyramid if you are working towards peak performance for your health and wellness.

Born into a culture where sleep is often cast aside as laziness and publicised as being a waste of time, this opinion is renowned with famous quotes such as 'sleep when you're dead'. It is safe to say sleep in society was – perhaps still is – classed as negative, when in actuality it is an underrated resource. It is a common misconception that individuals who lay in bed all day are slothful, so we try and instil habits by waking teenagers up earlier (who, if offered, would happily remain in bed till noon), yet when a baby sleeps, we are warned never to wake them. We are neglecting the value of sleep when it comes to children and young adults; this can affect their growth, attention, performance in school, and increase the likelihood of an injury.[1]

There are plenty of articles and conversations identifying why sleep is much more important than we originally thought it to be. Researchers like Dr Matthew Walker (an English scientist and professor of neuroscience and psychology at the University of California) and institutions like Berkely lead education and raise awareness around this subject. This wealth of information is why I wanted to include it as a separate chapter: it has certainly opened my eyes and piqued my interest when it comes to the topic of sleep.

There were moments where I found it extremely difficult to obtain quality sleep. I would wake up from a dream state and lie in bed contemplating events for hours. This time was used worrying, feeling anxious, and feeding negative thought patterns. When I needed to begin my day, I ended up feeling irritated and restless because of the lack of quality in my sleep. This impatient mindset continued throughout my working day. I knew my lack of sleep was affecting my performance because I couldn't process information as quickly or efficiently during the day, nor could I focus for longer periods of time.

My monkey mind[‡‡‡‡] was playing with me during the day as it would keep me awake in the early hours of the morning. I was aware nothing would change until I changed. My outlook on irregular sleep was to find a method which would displace the negative thoughts I was having. I wanted to push them out because I knew those morning hours lying awake contemplating would not change any situation I was concerned about. What I could change was my attitude. I sought to find a healthy avenue to change my thought process and aimed to navigate my energy towards digesting positive attitude videos. This gave me a healthier avenue of distraction, even though it included using social media before

---

[‡‡‡‡] This term refers to the restless, agitated state of mind that is often characterised by scattered thoughts, racing emotions, as well as a lack of focus or mental clarity. This state is often associated with anxiety, stress, and experiencing difficulty finding inner peace and/or calm. This term is derived from the Buddhist concept of 'Kapicitta'; referring to the restless, agitated state of mind constantly jumping from one thing to another, much like a monkey swinging from branch to branch.

bed, (this is clarified in the 'Time to Consider' section at the end of this chapter).

Tools that supported healthier sleep patterns included guided meditations, visualisations, and repeating positive affirmations. It provided distraction in the sense that I only had to focus and pay attention to one thing before I went to bed at night. This was the last thing I would do before I fell asleep. These tools enabled me to quieten my thoughts and drift off to sleep. I kept playing them throughout the night: this was intentional so that when I woke as predicted in the early hours, I was able to divert my attention towards the words that were still ringing around the room, instead of replaying events of possible outcomes in my head. This created an alternative state to focus on instead of defaulting to worrying or negative thinking. My attention was already focused on my sleep tools as soon as I was conscious enough to realise I'd woken up. Upon waking, those positive affirmations would continue to feed my brain in its wakeful state instead of letting my mind concentrate on my dream, worry about work, or fret about being up in the early hours. This method enabled me to breathe and calm my physical state back to a natural, neutral state in order for me to fall back asleep.

## What happens during sleep?

When your head hits the pillow, you may not fall asleep straight away (unless you are sleep deprived): you will linger between wakefulness and sleep (a bit like dozing, known as stage 1 sleep), which can last up to five minutes. When you lose consciousness, you enter stage 2 sleep; this is where your breathing slows, your muscles relax, your brain activity reduces, and your core body temperature drops.[2] Stage 3 is where deep sleep happens; your brain activity operates in delta waves. Stage 3 lasts up to 40 minutes; this is a vital stage of recovery. Think of it as your body getting its MOT. When stage 4 arises, you are typically 60–90 minutes into your sleep. In stage 4 your body will temporarily experience loss of muscle tone but your eyes will be moving rapidly beneath your eyelids. This stage is called REM or 'rapid eye movement' sleep. During REM your heart rate speeds up, breathing becomes irregular, and brain waves are more variable. REM stage sleep is associated with dreaming and memory consolidation.[3] It is also thought to enhance creativity and perceptual processing. You will repeat those four stages of sleep several times during the night.

**Sleep is money**
Allow me to now break down and debunk the common misconception of trying to make up sleep, especially for those who believe that they can use the weekend to top up the sleep they missed during the week.

Let's create a money box of sleep as an analogy, where you will invest in your sleep each night. You accumulate £1 for every hour of sleep per night. The money you gathered will be spent that following day; let's call this your energy expense. Every night you are back to zero before you enter the next evening's sleep. Sleep is profitable for that day's energy and many people mistake sleep as something as a hinderance to their work and therefore choose to forfeit sleep on the weekdays thinking they can make up the time on the weekend. This isn't possible: your cognition and physiology use sleep specifically to re-energise you for the following day.

Quality and quantity of sleep are not the same thing. There are many devices that can give you feedback into the quality of sleep you are getting versus the hours you spend in bed. You may be in bed, but you will not be sleeping the whole time. Your body's ability to wind down and then rise in the morning will alter the quality of sleep you are receiving.

There will be occasions where you will have trouble sleeping, leading to sleep inconsistency. You may lack quality sleep due to worry, stress, work deadlines, a newborn or teething baby, or school schedules. The below demonstrates what can typically happen during a sleep deprived week:

- £7 on Monday
- £4 on Tuesday
- £6 on Wednesday
- £7 on Thursday

- £6 on Friday
- £10 on Saturday
- £9 on Sunday

You may feel this is an even balance despite the low funds you provided on Tuesday because you input more funds on the weekend, correct? Accumulatively you saved and spent £49 on sleep that week. Now, if you were consistent with your spending, and instead placed £8 per night, every night, you could be benefiting from an extra £7 that week. This also demonstrates the extra £10 spent on the weekend did *not* make up for lost sleep during the week.

In reality it's more complex than this because it also depends on the energy you spent learning, exercising, creating, socialising etc. All these drain resources and deep sleep will support and vary according to what you have done during the previous day.

That exemplifies why it isn't possible to use the 'credit' you accumulate on the weekend to catch up on lost sleep. Technically, you only have one day to catch up on lost sleep: usually the Saturday because by Sunday you will need your body to return to its typical 'deprived' state for the week ahead, when you attempt to get to sleep at your usual weekday time. Catching up on that missed £7 will be difficult to do on the weekend, despite having spent more time in bed, because it takes longer than that for your body to recover. In fact, did you know it takes around four days to recover from one hour of lost sleep?[4] If we appropriate the money/debt metaphor, then you will constantly be in sleep debt. But – as I mentioned at the start of this chapter – sleep doesn't work like debt. It is determined by that day's exhaustion and accumulated stress.

Although there are standard recommendations on the hours of sleep each generation should be aiming for,[§§§§] it's important to remember that quality and quantity are not the

---

[§§§§] The recommended amount of sleep per night is: 7-9 hours for adults; 10–13 hours for children aged 3–5; 9–11 hours for children aged 6–13; and 8-10 hours for teenagers aged 14–17. However, the amount of sleep will vary according to individual needs, age, lifestyle, and overall health.

same thing and the key is to listen to your body. If you are hitting the pillow at night and falling asleep quickly, it's an indication of sleep deprivation. Similarly, if you are struggling to wake up in the morning, this is another sign you aren't getting enough sleep. These crucial insights allow you to understand and interpret how sleep affects your body and what hours are needed for you to function optimally. If you find you struggle to wake up to do your planned exercise that morning, it may be beneficial for your health and wellbeing to have an extra hour in bed. Perhaps you could try planning an early night if you desire to wake up earlier.

An overlooked problem in the world's obesity epidemic may be the alarm clock.[5] Professor Till Roenneberg studies 'social jet lag' – a chronic clash between what our bodies need (more sleep) and what our lives are demanding (being on time). Roenneberg et al. published a study on the sleep habits of 65,000 adults. Two-thirds experienced a one-hour disparity between how long they slept on workdays and weekends. The researchers found individuals who go to bed later but get up at the same time lose around 40 minutes of sleep on workdays. They are also spending less time outdoors. As I mentioned at the beginning of the chapter, sleep is viewed as an indulgence, but those who sleep fewer hours are not as efficient at their job. Our circadian clock controls a variety of functions, which includes body temperature, hormone secretion, and blood pressure.[*****]

Other studies also suggest a lack of sleep causes higher secretions of ghrelin,[†††††] an appetite hormone, as well as a

---

[*****] The circadian clock is a natural internal system that regulates your sleep-wake cycle. It also influences behavioural and physiological processes. This is influenced by external cues such as light and temperature. Disruptions to your circadian clock (such as those on shift work or when you experience jet lag) can have negative effects on individuals' health and wellbeing. Exposure to sunlight and getting enough sleep helps the rhythm of this clock run smoothly.

[†††††] Ghrelin is a hormone produced by cells in the stomach. This is often referred to as the 'hunger hormone' because its levels rise before meals (increasing the drive to eat) and then fall after eating.

reduction of leptin,[‡‡‡‡‡] the satiety hormone. Roenneberg states for every hour of social jet lag accrued, the risk of being overweight or obese increases by 33%.[5]

A study by Matthew Christensen from the University of California reported that night-time exposure to smartphone screens is associated with lower sleep quality, based on the use of a smartphone 60 minutes before bedtime.[6] Christian's team collated 653 adults' sleeping hours and quality across the United States of America. On average, he found participants activated his or her phone for a total of 4 minutes every 60 minutes, within a 24-hour period. Longer quantities of daily screen time use were associated with poor sleep and less sleep overall.

Russell Johnson et al. at Michigan State University surveyed a spectrum of workers in the United States of America who used their phone for business as it is increasing productivity in knowledge-based work.[7] Eighty-two upper-level managers were studied every day for two weeks. The study showed using their smartphones at night for business purposes cut into their sleep and sapped their energy the following workday. Not only were they tired, but they were also less engaged – in comparison to their peers who unplugged their phones. Johnson describes smartphones as 'perfectly designed to disrupt sleep'. After all, if their aim is to mentally engage us so we carry on engaging late into the evening, this increases difficulty for individuals to detach from work in order to relax and fall asleep.

Although we know sleep has many benefits and it's necessary for us humans, we still push the boundaries of sleep and become sleep deprived: we are exhausted, irritated, and prone to mental and physical illnesses. We also lose productivity: the one thing many people are striving for in their waking day! According to a marketing survey from a

---

[‡‡‡‡‡] Leptin is a hormone produced by fat cells: its primary role is to regulate appetite and metabolism. Leptin levels are typically higher in individuals with a healthy weight and lower in individuals who are overweight or obese.

mattress company, individuals rack up 30 hours of sleep debt a month![2]

It is suggested that most adults require approximately nine hours' sleep per night, yet the invention of the light bulb and advances in technology have hampered and delayed the time we would usually get to bed – which used to be when the sun sets. Stress, caffeine, and shift work has also contributed to Brits getting less sleep. According to a YouGov poll, 47% aren't sure sleep would improve their life; 24% would eliminate the need for sleep if they had the choice; and 59% go to bed at 11 p.m. or later. Yet 59% don't think they get enough sleep per night.[8] In fact, Brits get less than six hours' sleep per night and up to a quarter of people use sleeping pills. What I find unsurprising is that the British Economy loses £30bn a year because of sleep loss.[8]

The most fascinating part of *why* we need so much sleep and what exactly happens to our brain during sleep is still a mystery. There are countless studies on the benefits of sleep and neuroscientist Dr Matthew Walker delves into explanations of what can happen if we do not prioritise sleep in his book *Why We Sleep*.[9] We are told sleep regulates our mood (I can most certainly vouch for that when I don't get a good night's kip!) and it is related to our learning and memory functions. But how is it critical to our health, weight, and energy levels? Do we get better sleep from exercising or does exercise enable us to sleep well?

**Sleep and exercise**
Even though exercise has been associated with better sleep, research shows poor sleep contributes to low levels of physical activity. If we sleep poorly, we are less likely to put in a good workout, yet that is exactly what is needed in order to sleep well. As mentioned earlier, there can be reasons for disturbed sleep. However, some of these are more chronic. 'Sleep disorder' refers to difficulties in falling asleep, staying asleep, feeling fatigue during the day, difficulty concentrating, and experiencing trouble breathing. This includes a person's brain failing to properly control breathing during sleep.

Suffering this type of disturbance during sleep can lead to hypertension, heart disease, mood, and memory problems.[10]

One-third of all adults report complaints of inadequate sleep due to a common disorder called 'sleep apnoea'. Eighteen million people in the United States of America have sleep apnoea. In the United Kingdom 45% are estimated to be living with obstructive sleep apnoea and around 2–4% of the UK population has sleep apnoea. Research conducted by the Office of Health Economics for the British Lung Foundation states that awareness, diagnosis, and treatment could save the National Health Service (NHS) up to £28 million as well as prevent up to 40,000 road traffic accidents per year.[11]

The Sleep Foundation claim those who suffer from sleep apnoea are usually overweight. Since daytime sleepiness lowers energy levels, a vicious cycle occurs where tired sufferers of sleep apnoea will be less motivated to do the exercise they so desperately need to help treat this type of condition. Reid et al., (using a sample containing older adults with insomnia) found four months of aerobic exercise training significantly improved sleep quality. It also reduced daytime sleepiness and depressive symptoms.[12, 13] The significance of this shows that (1) it is not an overnight fix and (2) the *consistency* of exercise allowed the subjects to increase their sleep by 1.25 hours per night more than their non-exercise counterparts.

Those who do not get enough sleep also have a bigger appetite. Leptin levels decrease and appetite levels increase. Psychological manifestations of fatigue, sleep, and hunger are similar: therefore, when you feel sleepy you may experience the urge to go to the fridge instead of heading to bed.[10]

A large-scale observational study by Wennman et al. examined the relationship between sleep and different motivations for exercise.[14] If exercise was for leisure, occupational purposes, or transportation, those who slept best tended to be engaging in higher amounts of leisure and physical activity. The opposite was true for those who performed higher levels of occupational physical activity or no exercise at all; they were more likely to have experienced poor sleep.[14] Siddarth et al. tested groups participating in aerobic exercise and mind-body exercises such as yoga and tai chi.[14] The findings were conclusive: all forms of exercise produced better sleep quality (measured by PSQI scores)[§§§§§] but Siddarth et al. found those individuals who participated in mind-body exercises were in a significantly better mood, and experienced improved mental health and sleep compared to those individuals who had participated in aerobic exercise alone.

Dr Loren Fishman speaks about yoga being able to thicken layers of cerebral cortex; increasing neuroplasticity, enabling us to learn new ideas and change the way we do things. Neuroscience behind yoga explains why it is so effective in reducing stress and creating balance in the body: because yoga involves mindful and controlled movements. It is recorded that our brain likes yoga as there is a strong correlation between the activity within the prefrontal cortex and this is highlighted when attempting to maintain your concentration and stillness. Stimulation of the parasympathetic nervous system increases during the process of restoration and healing, which is responsible for calming us down.[15]

Sleep deficiency is linked to feelings of frustration, worry, or being cranky in social situations. If you notice sleep isn't easy for you there may be a positive twist that you can adopt into your life. A positive thinking study split 102 subjects into three groups: the first was given a visualisation task (to visualise a positive outcome to their worries); the second group was given verbal positive outcomes; and the last group was given instructions to visualise any positive image whenever they started to worry.[16] Those groups who visualised a positive image, whether it related to a specific

---

[§§§§§] The Pittsburgh Sleep Quality Index (PSQI) is a self-reported questionnaire used to assess the quality of a person's sleep. The score determines the overall quality of a person's sleep and is often used in research studies in different populations. It can also be used by healthcare providers to diagnose and treat sleep disorders.

worry or not, reported greater happiness. They were more restful and found to have decreased their levels of anxiety. Taking an intention and using it to serve positive habits means you are taking action towards the problem in front of you. This isn't stating the fact you need to 'stay positive' per se; this is picking apart things that you can control such as your inner state of happiness, no matter what is going on around you.

For me, re-writing my inner dialogue and changing my attitude of how I perceived difficult situations meant there was room for growth. This worked for me because social media provided a distraction in the right way and it allowed me to navigate away from the countless repetitive thoughts that did not serve me. I was also aware this was depleting my energy. I continue to use these practices to this day, but I alternate between online affirmations, videos, and music (using a sleep timer). I have formed the habit of meditating before bed which allows me to settle my thoughts, and relax my nervous system and muscles. These days, it is extremely rare that I wake up in the middle of the night with restless thoughts. Should this happen, I simply go back to the habits I created such as using breathwork and guided meditation practices.

I noticed significant changes in relation to the quality of sleep since I set a boundary when it came to using my phone late at night. The positive difference I experienced when I stopped using my phone an hour before bed was staggering. Since that realisation this habit has become an asset towards experiencing a great night's sleep: I reinforce and advocate such behaviour change for myself and my clients who have trouble sleeping. This shift towards a better night's sleep created a healthier habit and changed my attitude towards relaxation and winding down, as well as building boundaries for my health and wellbeing.

If you are suffering or think you may be suffering from a sleep disorder, it's recommended you seek medical advice. This can make the difference between every part of your wellbeing collapsing or thriving. Getting enough sleep enables you to function well, you are likely to make smarter decisions, as well as stay alert and engaged for longer periods of time. You will find you are far more creative and can maintain a higher level of concentration where needed. Although Thomas Edison, America's greatest inventor, liked to boast about how little he slept at night he failed to mention how much he napped during the day! His associate even said his 'genius for sleep equalled his genius for invention'.

There may be some sacrifices and routines that need to be adapted regarding your sleep, but the key is to assess what means more to you in the moment, and what you seek for yourself in the long term. The choice you make will either lead to another step forward towards your personal success – be it weight loss, career progress, or a happier, more fulfilled life – or it will leave you stuck in a position where you haven't made any forward gains towards the things you desire. When you are accountable regarding your daily decisions and form positive, actionable habits for your health, energy, and productivity this will aid and support your happiness and success. Bear in mind, what works for one person may not work in your favour. The best tool will be in discovering what works for you, your lifestyle, and schedule, as well as what priorities you have. That is your mission.

## TIME TO CONSIDER

1) **Set yourself a timer**
   If you are the type of person who is on social media before bed, you may not realise the amount blue light emitted by your phone suppresses your body's release of melatonin.****** Melatonin is released gradually as darkness falls but artificial light disturbs the release of this hormone, so one reason you may find it hard to fall asleep straight away is because the sleep hormone's release has been disrupted. The blue light your eyes are absorbing keeps your brain alert and suppresses the body's chemical

---

****** Melatonin is a hormone produced naturally by the body. It helps regulate sleep-wake cycles and is involved in the body's internal circadian clock.

release that triggers the need for sleep. Despite many phones having a sleep filter or buying novelty items such as blue light filtering glasses, may not be nearly as powerful or impactful as actually leaving your phone alone 60–90 minutes before bed.

Set a timer to start an hour before you plan to go to sleep. Any time leading up to then is your chance to catch up with friends online, work emails, family phone calls, etc. before your bedtime countdown starts. When your one-hour timer begins, activate 'Do Not Disturb' on your phone and get ready for restful sleep. This purposeful one-hour timer will enable you to wind down and set a routine before bed. Such things can include brushing your teeth or locking any doors: the customary things you do before bed. If you find you have a lot of time left before you need to fall asleep, you may opt to read a book or magazine, talk to your partner, meditate, or sit in stillness.

Media has prevented us from being still or bored and this is a great time to get some space and reduce the time you are taking in new information. It can also provide you with time to settle down your thoughts and enter stillness before sleep. Breathwork also aids your body and mind in preparing for sleep: taking in full deep breaths is crucial for falling into a restful, relaxed sleep.

2) **Switch off your phone**
We are naturally drawn to our phone. Have you noticed even if your phone is on silent you may think you have heard an alert, or worse, seen one and then when you check your phone you realise it was a figment your imagination? This is how much we rely on our 'third hand' aka, our phone: It is attached to us during every waking moment. By regaining control and making time to switch your phone off, although it will take discipline and practice, it will benefit your mental health in the long run.

3) **Electronic-free zones**
Many people do not sleep next to their phone, let alone have it in the same room. There are many individuals who

claim to not only live by the rule of turning off all electronic devices before sleep, but they enforce a boundary that ensures all electronics are removed from the bedroom.

Create technology-free zones in your home. This could include the dinner table or bedroom. It will allow you and your family to have quality personal time and prevents technology interrupting those special moments within your life.

### 4) Abstinence

Abstain from caffeine from around noon and avoid alcohol in the evening because both are stimulants. Caffeine is said to remain in your bloodstream for up to ten hours, which means a mocha at 4 p.m. will still be present in your bloodstream at night and could be the cause of your restlessness. Alcohol triggers fragmented sleep, insomnia, and other possible serious sleep issues.[17] Alcohol before bed has also been linked to closing your airway whilst asleep which increases sleep apnoea; it also decreases melatonin levels.

### 5) Walk it out

Something I wish I'd known earlier was: if you cannot get to sleep and you are lying in bed waiting for sleep to come, get out of bed. Go and relax in another room and come back to bed later when you feel sleepy again. Dr Matthew Walker suggests if sleep is elusive after 25 minutes of lying in bed, walk it out.

### 6) Do nothing

Everyone will have experienced an occasion where they had a bad night's sleep: if you are unfortunate to have one, do nothing!

Follow the guidelines set out above but do not go to bed earlier that following night. The American Academy of Sleep Medicine and the Sleep Research Society presented a study which found people who turned in early, slept in later, or took naps to compensate for a night (or nights) of tossing and turning were more likely to go from acute insomnia to chronic insomnia instead of back to normal, healthy sleep.[18] So do nothing if you've had a bad night's kip. Keep following your routine.

7) **Journal / write**
Journaling or writing is another way to use the time before bed to record all the things you have discovered during your day. It can provide a reminder of all the good things you have accomplished. Perhaps write down who and what you are grateful for; this will also increase your state of happiness before bed, which consequently raises the chances for you to sustain a healthier, happier attitude in life.

## CHAPTER TEN: I AM GRATEFUL FOR YOU

*Gratitude can transform common days into thanksgiving,
turn routine jobs into joy,
and change ordinary opportunities into blessings.*
*Proverb*[1]

The one thing many people who are negative have in common, and love to do, is complain. Some may call these types of personalities pessimists, or realists. Typically, an optimist will advocate that there is positivity found in anything and everything – you simply need to look for it (you may recall many ways to remain optimistic in chapter five). Individuals who experience overall happiness tend to be more positive and have one clear defining thing in common: gratitude. This common foundation brings them awareness via practising the art of gratitude and grounding them in the current moment. By no means does it diminish their need to achieve more, but it shines the light on the abundant things or people they already have within their life. Those who are extremely ambitious and successful tend to be appreciative with what they have, all the while maintaining high aspirations within their professional or personal domain. Being grateful is an avenue that allows people to account for all the wonderful things they have in the present moment, as well as being fully content and happy now.

For me, gratitude began years ago, when I read how we *should* be more grateful for things we have in life. I do not recall ever being given an explanation or rationale as to *why* we should be grateful, but I do recall being advised this is a game changer: it is a key thing to incorporate if you wish to experience more feelings such as happiness, fulfilment, and pleasure. This is why I included a chapter on gratitude: to expand on things that have already been published and delve deeper into the reasons behind being more grateful, as well as the wider impact on our health, wellbeing, happiness, and success.

I adore writing my thoughts and feelings down on paper. When I feel alone or want nothing more than to be by myself, in my own thoughts, I take pen to paper and describe what I am feeling. This is my personal sanctuary; reflective journaling. This tool enables me to track my feelings and it meant I became more self-aware assessing my own emotions. I recall a conversation with a close friend, who mentioned how I had the ability to overcome hardships easily. In their opinion, I represented a strong person. However, I will admit that comment came somewhat as a surprise at the time, and made me question where this came from.

My family have a history of strong female characters, yet we never shared stories of what this entailed. Both sides of my family also have a history of depression – this was never openly discussed nor was I fully aware of it. One morning the impact of depression shook our family to its very core. I had been told about my dear cousin who took his own life at the age of nineteen. I was only fourteen at the time so I couldn't quite fathom the journey he would have taken that led him down this dark path. I recall leaving school early for the funeral; the first funeral I remember attending.

As I travelled to the mortuary with my family, I remember being engulfed with fury. It is a feeling I will never forget. I was distraught that my wonderful, funny, easy-going, kind cousin took his own life, which for some of us was a complete shock. There were many who had not known how much he was suffering; we were left in the dark about his pain that was now seemingly obvious. Now here I was with my family and all I could feel was a surge of anger towards him. I was furious and I blamed him. My exact thoughts were, *You took the easy way out.*

My thoughts were influenced by my own personal suffering. At that time I was battling with thoughts of taking my own life. His death emphasised how much he'd been hurting; it also made me see how heartbroken our family was, including myself. I was heartbroken for my family and the lack of attention anyone had paid towards his pain, and heartbroken for my own internal pain I was conflicted with. I could not explain where my internal strength began or how it was nurtured; all I knew was he took his life and it was, and will always be, a reminder that no matter how hard it gets, I couldn't do it. I saw first-hand the grief around me and how much my family suffered for days, months, and years after his death.

This is one reason why journaling came as an aid. When I felt alone and did not know whom to speak to, I developed ways that strengthened my emotional intelligence and self-reflection and also nurtured the support I most needed during difficult times. I gradually sought ways that could distract me from my painful inner dialogue: that was when I actively nurtured the skill of gratitude. For a period, after I would journal, I would write down five things I was grateful for every evening. There were days when I found this to be a difficult task, particularly when I was feeling rather negative and downhearted. Despite the struggle, I continued to list things I was grateful for. I actively sought things in my current state that were abundant. In the face of my personal battles, I sought to find hope during moments of despair. This practice served as a reminder that I could ground myself in the moment by reflecting on positive factors. I continue to practise gratitude to this day because what I learnt through this was self-compassion, centring, and joy. Although I experienced many short-term and long-term benefits because of my gratitude practice, for a long time I never understood why – until now.

## What is gratitude?

Gratitude originally derived from the Latin *gratus*, meaning 'pleasing' or 'thankful'. Its modern meaning encompasses grace, graciousness, or gratefulness. Gratitude is a thankful appreciation for what an individual receives; whether tangible or intangible. Expressing gratitude allows people to acknowledge all that is good within their lives. Many people are constantly moving forwards while others are constantly reflecting on the past events. Yet how many of us stop to think about how far we have come, or what we have managed to accomplish thus far in our lives? For many who are goal-orientated, it can be unusual to pause and reflect before hastily moving on to the next task or target. Many of us are often too preoccupied with wanting more and get caught up in chasing the next adventure, and using this to define the thing that will make us happy. This indefinite pursuit of happiness is an ever-evolving mirage as we continue to work towards that reward. When was the last time you paused to be truly appreciative and grateful for everything you already have in your life?

Gratitude is a powerful human emotion; it is a way to acknowledge good things in life. We usually experience this when we receive unexpected gifts from a stranger. (As long it is something you want and not just a gift of convention such as Christmas presents). This experience of giving and receiving enables both parties to enjoy this exchange of gratitude. Simply put, feeling this emotion puts both parties in a good mood. For the receiver, they acknowledge they are considered and thought about. For the giver, they experience the pleasure of accepting gratitude. The pleasure you will see when you have given the perfect gift brings you a powerful emotion. Take, for example, giving a small gift to a child; their expression alone will enable you to feel good because their pleasure and emotions are obvious. They do not care about how their reaction is perceived (an unfortunate trait adults pick up with age). When you contribute to that state of happiness and emotion it can be multiplied in abundance without having to break your bank balance!

*Gratitude is associated with a personal benefit that was not intentionally sought after, deserved, or earned but rather because of the good intentions of another person.*
Emmons and McCullough[2]

The parasympathetic nervous system increases when we are grateful and there is plenty of research that has shown reductions in stress and an increase in wellbeing. Stress hormones such as cortisol are 23% lower in people who are grateful and in those who practise gratitude daily.[‡] Being grateful may also reduce the effects of brain ageing. Those who practised gratitude presented better cardiac functioning and were more resilient when encountering emotional setbacks and negative experiences.[2] The hypothalamus – which regulates appetite, sleep, temperature, metabolism, and growth – is activated when we feel gratitude and present when there are acts of kindness.[3]

Gratitude also floods our brains with dopamine; a chemical messenger that affects movement, emotions, and the ability to experience pleasure and pain. When the feeling of gratitude feeds this chemical signal, it gives individuals a natural high; similar to that experience of receiving praise for your efforts during a difficult project at work. Neural mechanisms that are responsible for feelings of gratitude evoke the right anterior cortex.[1] These signal moral judgements to the brain, involving feelings of gratefulness.

The brain structure of those who express and feel more gratitude contains a higher volume of grey matter. Those associated with this increased quantity of grey matter involves detailed perceptual processing in social cognition.[4] All these effects of gratitude, if practised daily, can produce longer lasting feelings of happiness and contentment. Conscious and constant gratitude practice releases neurotransmitters which allow these pathways to increase in strength and create a permanent grateful and positive nature within us.[2] Alex Korb explains how the brain loves confirmation bias and searches for things that prove what you already believe to be true.

---

[‡] Cortisol is produced by the adrenal gland in response to stress. It plays several important roles in the body, including regulating metabolism, immune function, and blood pressure. Cortisol can be influenced by a number of factors including sleep, exercise, and emotional states. High levels of this hormone can cause negative health effects such as weight gain, low immune function, and reduced cognitive performance.

When you start to be grateful, your brain will seek more things to be grateful for.[5] When someone worries about adverse outcomes the brain is wired to focus only on the negative information. Yet when practising gratitude, we train the brain to select positive emotions and thoughts. Korb says our brain cannot focus on positive *and* negative information at the same time. Positive emotions and thoughts reduce anxiety and feelings of apprehension.

**Gratitude and crisis**
Gratitude plays a significant role when encountering major trauma or stress. Khasdan et al. looked at Vietnam War veterans with and without post-traumatic stress disorder (PTSD). Through examining associations with gratitude and wellbeing over time, this was proven to have a unique association with each dimension of wellbeing in both groups.[6] Gratitude was also a major contributor to resilience following the terrorist attacks on 9/11.[7] Positive emotions experienced in the wake of this attack that included love, interest, and gratitude accounted for relations between resilience and the development of depressive symptoms. In their findings it was suggested that positive emotions buffer resilient people against depression; recognising all that you can be thankful for – even during the worst times – fosters resilience. Individuals who sought mental guidance felt better and recovered sooner. The group who had written letters of gratitude alongside their regular counselling sessions benefitted the most. Those who were asked to journal their negative experiences (instead of writing a gratitude letter) reported increased feelings of anxiety and depression.

**Gratitude and wellbeing**
When patients were asked to keep a gratitude journal, 16% of subjects reported a reduction in symptoms and 10% noted reductions in physical pain. It also enhanced their personal motivation to exercise (particularly important as this can enhance benefits towards a patient's recovery).[8]

In addition to these psychological benefits, practising gratitude improves our physical wellbeing. According to

Emmons, those who keep a gratitude journal are more likely to have a 25% reduction in dietary fat intake. It has also been found that writing in a gratitude journal improves sleep – which is significant now you know how poor sleep compromises wellbeing. A study on self-help interventions involving university students found 41 participants (32 female) improved their sleep when comparing it to their baseline by being grateful; it helped students quieten their minds and sleep better.[9] Gratitude increases the quality of your sleep, decreases the time it takes to fall asleep, and lengthens the duration of sleep.[9]

This in turn brings about a positive domino effect: gratitude improves our sleep quality which supports your wellbeing (such as reductions in stress, anxiety, depression, and physiological pain, boosting the overall immune system). Emmons and McCullough conducted another study in which one group was asked to record things they were grateful for during the week, whereas another group of participants had to write down everything that displeased them. A third group wrote about events affecting them, with no emphasis on either positive or negative aspects. The findings were that those who were most grateful had reported an increased amount of happiness and joy, as well as fewer symptoms of physical illnesses. These participants spent more time exercising and felt more optimism within their lives, as well as an increased state of positivity. They were also more likely to offer emotional support to others, meaning their personal wellbeing expanded to increasing connections with others.[8]

**Gratitude and success**
An expression of gratitude helps build sustaining long-term relationships and improves interpersonal relationships at home and work.[2] A study that included couples who expressed their gratitude via being thankful to one another found their relationships were often sustained with mutual trust and loyalty, and they had long-lasting relationships. Gratitude positively affects both personal and professional relationships. Many organisations have begun to consider this crucial to employees' efficiency, success, and productivity, as

well as positively influencing organisational behaviours. It improves relationships, social support, workers' wellbeing, and overall positivity, as well as reducing negative emotions in the workplace.[10] Algoe found expressing gratitude in the workplace was a proactive action towards building interpersonal bonds and triggered feelings of closeness.[11] Those who expressed gratitude were more likely to volunteer for assignments and be willing to take the extra steps for accomplishing tasks, as well as being happier to work as part of a team.

Employers who thanked their staff and employees for the work they do found those individuals worked harder and were increasingly motivated. Researchers at Wharton School of the University of Pennsylvania randomly divided fundraisers into two groups. One group made phone calls to solicit donations and the second, assigned to another day, received a pep talk from the director of annual giving. The group who was given a pep talk made 50% more fundraising calls than the other, who did not receive this pep talk. This unique tool provided employees with an extra boost of motivation to work harder and be more productive, even though they were already carrying out good deeds.[12]

**Gratitude and happiness**

*Be thankful for what you have; you'll end up having more. If you concentrate on what you don't have, you will never have enough.*

*Oprah Winfrey*

Psychologist Martin Seligman asked 411 participants to write and personally deliver a letter of gratitude to those who had been especially kind to them but had not had a chance to thank them properly. Findings showed they were instantly happier, *and* these benefits were maintained for a month after their initial gratitude visit.[13]

Gratitude and its connection to happiness reveals voluntary expressions of joy. When you are appreciated, thanked, or given kind words, usually this experience will lead to a smile spreading across your face. One of the reasons will be because your brain is responding to and reflecting the increasing number of positive emotions you are experiencing.

Throughout this book I have touched on self-compassion: gratitude forms an important part of this because by including and practising gratitude we enable ourselves to celebrate our individual achievements. When we acknowledge what we have accomplished and what others have accomplished, we appreciate the support received thus far and can truly revel in the wonder of thankfulness. We are thankful for what has come before us as well as being able to capture everything we are thankful for in this moment. Some people tend to recognise the source of such goodness lies outside themselves; this is not seeking happiness elsewhere, rather it is about helping people connect to something larger than themselves. Whether this is connecting to other people, nature, or a higher power, being thankful, or appreciating all the good that is present now will bring an increased sense of happiness within.

Below are a few examples of ways you can enable yourself to create a happier and healthier way of living. By being a little grateful every day you are enhancing your wellbeing, forging stronger connections, and building resilience. Gratitude is not limited to what you have in the moment, it can evolve from everything you have been through, your mindset, and your support network. Some individuals may experience resistance here and can find it initially challenging to be grateful; remember the mind is great at cycling old habits and forging new ones will take purposeful and conscious effort at the beginning.

When you begin to open yourself up and develop a grateful mindset, the negative moments will exist few and far between, and you will start to see challenges, problems, and situations from a redefined frame of reference. This newfound perspective will bring both clarity and new lessons within the moment because you are dealing with the situation as well as being present. Thinking in a broader perspective, everything has brought you to this point right here: reading this book alone means you are taking steps to forge new pathways for your own happiness. This is also a healthy reminder that you serve a purpose and you can continue to move forward despite the circumstances around you.

Practising gratitude or expressing gratefulness to others will raise your levels of happiness. It may be a spouse, parent, sibling, or your children. It can encompass your freedom; the country you live in, the time you spend by yourself, or your life in general. It can include being grateful about the materials you acquired; your car, your house, your job, or the holidays you go on. It can even involve things such as past events, elements of your childhood, or your current surroundings: the list is endless.

## TIME TO CONSIDER

1) **A gratitude journal**
   Begin by being grateful each day. Start with writing down five things you are grateful for every evening. Try to do this before you go to bed because you will be able to reflect on your day. This will enable you to make peace with everything you may have encountered (including the challenges) and you will be able to acknowledge lessons learnt along the way.

   By taking time to account for all things you are grateful for, you will be able to rest more peacefully. Those who practise gratitude last thing at night and first thing in the morning tend to experience significantly better sleep and a happier outlook for the day ahead.

   To value the full benefits in your wellbeing, try this activity for 21 days, this may not be enough to form a new habit but is achievable. As you develop this into a habit you will be able to notice positive changes, and reflect how this activity has added to your overall sense of wellbeing and happiness.

2) **Capture the moment**
   Demonstrate gratitude and take a picture of one thing you are grateful for each day. Try doing this for 30 days. Once the 30 days are up, you can create collage of shots you

have collected. This is another moment that will enable you to be grateful for the entire month as you reflect your accumulated gratitude pictures laid in front of you.

3) **Send a loving message**
Send someone a message detailing three reasons why you appreciate them. This is such a beautiful exchange of loving moments and it can be useful to strengthen your relationships.

If you experience some trepidation about sending something so abruptly, you could preface the message so they can understand its context. Something as simple as: 'I wanted to spread a little more love and kindness into the world; with that in mind I wanted to send you three things I appreciate about you ...'

Ensure these are specific and personal messages for the individual to showcase that you appreciate them. Do not expect anything back but send it out for your own wellbeing and you will notice the effects days and months after, particularly when you recall the event.

Personal note: When I did this activity with a few family members and friends, despite sending them with a feeling of apprehension, I did not expect answers to flood back detailing why they were grateful for me. When I received reciprocal messages of their love for me, this unexpected turn enabled me to triple my sense of contentment and happiness because it was the unexpected gift filling my emotions, as mentioned earlier in this chapter. Another significant feeling is that, despite this happening years ago, the same feeling of comfort, joy, and happiness fill my senses whenever I recall the event. That experience continues to give me pleasure in positivity, unconditional love, and gratitude for that moment.

4) **Write a letter**
Write a letter of gratitude to someone on how they have made a difference to you or helped you in any way. You may think back to a time when someone gave you helpful

advice or support when you were going through a difficult time. It could be a letter to someone you felt wronged you in some way but could not confront at the time. This can be a challenge if you have not healed from the trauma of the event, but it can also give you a giant step towards forgiveness and releasing any residual resentment you may hold towards them.

Personal note: When I wrote a letter of gratitude to someone who broke my heart (which turned out to be breaking my personal expectations and not my heart) I acknowledged my need to please and unwillingness to create boundaries. The words came so easily to me because they were from the heart and because enough time had passed to guide me towards forgiveness rather than anger. In this letter I wrote all the things I thought he was to me and how I felt. I also explored the reasons why I was thankful for the experiences – both good and bad. Months down the line I remember seeing the draft on my computer; I felt proud I was able to be kind to this person despite the considerable hurt I'd experienced. Although I had no intention to send it (as I had chosen to cut off contact with this person) this task gave me a chance to clip the strings of attachment and release the relationship in a healthier way. It felt freeing and gave me the relief and resolution I needed.

5) **A moment to give back**
Do something nice for someone, without telling anyone what you did. In today's world social media publicises everything we do; however, if you do something sincerely without the need for credit or acknowledgement, this is a true sense of giving. Gratitude without egotism can be a powerful tool as you are doing a good deed without seeking recognition or validation.

➢ Can you pay it forwards for the person behind you?
➢ Are you able to send someone a gift without them knowing it was you?

## 6) Wake up in gratitude

Spend just five minutes in the morning going through the things you are grateful for before the day has begun. Everything you are grateful for in that moment.

The true sense of happiness involves being in the present: you need to let go of the pretence that you must earn your happiness. There is no need to force happiness to be a reward; allow it to be a feeling and learn to embrace happiness no matter the circumstances. Being happy is a choice and whether you are experiencing a good or bad event in your life, you can still be internally happy.

I have noticed when I need to refocus on being in the present moment, nothing makes me come back to a present state of positivity quicker than reminding myself of all the things I can be grateful for. Gratitude has been by far the most rewarding tool to navigate myself into the present moment. I appreciate this more because I remind myself that every state is temporary, and it will soon pass. Being grateful broadens our experience of happiness, so why not increase your levels of happiness by practising gratitude?

*It is not happiness that brings us gratitude.*
*It is gratitude that brings us happiness.*
                                                              Unknown

## CHAPTER ELEVEN: THE STORM WILL PASS

*Life isn't supposed to be easy. When you have your toughest challenges, your most trying moments usually come before your greatest success.*
Tulshi Varsani

Have you ever considered a moment in time when everything changed? It can be described as a defining moment in your life: one you can recall with vivid detail, which also brings about a surge of emotions you experienced that day. Many people know exactly where they were during 9/11 or how they heard about Princess Diana's passing. Big moments in time often transport you back to a memory ingrained in your mind; it is increasingly difficult to forget them. We all have this within our lives. This is one of mine.

I was going about my usual routine on a crisp January morning – managing responsibilities, creating projects, and juggling various work commitments – when our team was introduced to a new manager. I was feeling a touch apprehensive but brushed it off as quickly as it came into existence. I reassured myself that it was exciting to have more support. A few days passed and my apprehension returned. I'm unsure why we often dismiss this intuitive feeling: I have since come to understand that it should be nurtured. Such feelings are necessary before we encounter problems because it holds a warning, it can be identified as the first red flag. Those signals from your body to your brain are important indicators, yet many choose to dismiss them until hard evidence is apparent. Unfortunately, there are times we mistrust our body's manifestation of this type of communication because we may have decided our brain needs more proof, which can often lead to biases we generate to either support or dismiss how we are thinking or feeling.

During my introductory meetings with this new team member, I was spoken to in a stern, direct, and formal manner, which was vastly different to how I was treated by them in public. Next came evidence of meetings behind my back about me, and lack of communication was evident. This was the time I knew to trust my gut because there was one moment which I can recall as if it happened only yesterday.

Sitting in an open area in a I, I had that feeling again. I can remember feeling six inches tall. The conversation was as blunt and stern as all my other encounters; it felt as if I was being interviewed for my position. At this point I had been in my role for 19 months, during which I'd been working on understanding, adapting, trusting, and developing matters into something worth nurturing; something bigger than me. A few weeks passed from that initial 'interview' experience I was asked to arrange a time for another one-to-one. Yet again I was filled with confusion which evolved into a feeling of dread and disappointment. I can still recall that feeling as if experiencing the whole event again. I sat there thinking, *I am about to fall and there is nothing around me to grab on to*. I could not stop myself from cascading down a deep hole and slipping into darkness. The new team member, a person whom I was told would support me, gave me the news in no uncertain terms that they would be leading my numerous projects and all decisions should be passed by them before moving forwards.

If I am honest, I felt as if I had been slapped in the face. I loved everything I was developing; it ignited passion, enthusiasm, and happiness in the roles and responsibilities I held. So, in an attempt to catch my breath after this information, I remained calm and professional, and I just sat there. It felt as if every bone in my body went limp and I could not move. All I could do was blink and stare ahead into an abyss. Inside I was devastated and heartbroken, but I would not let any of these emotions be visible. Every moment I'd spent pushing myself, working long hours and dedicating my time and energy into the role, everything I had been developing seemed to have slipped away with me in this pit and I sat there by myself, alone. Back then I was someone who used to take things to heart, so I immediately wondered what went wrong, stumbling over questions and personal reflections on what I had been doing for the past 19 months. A flood of negativity and self-doubt brought questions such as, *Was I not good enough?* And, *What more could I have done?*

This unexpected blow arrived after a lot of time was spent focused on my mindset, this new challenge brought in an opportunity. A circumstance that enabled me to reframe into a positive change.

Let me take you back to 19 months before this moment, when I first embarked on this role. If you remember, in chapter two I spoke about the multitude of feelings I was experiencing at the time. I can only describe those moments as fumbling around in the dark, attempting to find my own way. I had no friends or family around me; instead I had a career in an industry I appreciated and valued. Over the course of several months (and thanks to my friend's invaluable intervention) I was able to find myself in a space where I felt worthy, had a sense of belonging, and had created a safe environment around me.

As a child, I recall being quite shy. I was extremely imaginative and loved playing by myself in my delusional happy space, where I would create my own adventures. In adulthood, there were many moments where I would find myself transported back to that familiar childhood feeling of shyness, particularly when I was told by a person of the opposite sex to sit down and shut up. In those moments I would merge back into those familiar shadows: I would bite my tongue and let others lead. I experienced other roles within my career where I was told to stay silent, say nothing and just deal with the situation. During such meetings I instantly felt six inches tall and immediately reverted to the role of a quiet, shy little girl who could not stand up for herself.

Such moments became enormously familiar during the year that new person joined our team. I would see the team laughing and joking whilst I worked with clients, which felt like a trigger for me. These moments were familiar to me as a child where I recalled seeing the other kids laughing and playing without me. It brought back feelings of being excluded and believing I was the odd one out. I decided this was simply one of my known insecurities, so I brushed aside any indifferences and delved deeper into my work and condensed responsibilities.

Even though this new manager's decision meant I had far less accountability within my role, I made it a choice to do the best I could with what I had. I enjoyed being busy and this was particularly useful (but not healthy) for blocking out any emotions I needed to confront. Instead, I would keep my feelings to myself and hide what I was truly experiencing inside and suppressed what I actually thought:

*What an injustice! How can someone come in and take over with no contemplation of how things are? How can someone come in and change the rules based on the game they wanted to play? Why is it some men feel they need to exert their power and make others feel so small?*

The little girl inside of me simply saw this as a familiar pattern, where her favourite toy was snatched away. I was left feeling defeated and decided to bow out of the battle that faced me.

Throughout that following year, because I was in a space where there was a lack of purposeful work I sought challenges elsewhere, something that could push me intellectually. Driven by demotivating conversations and feelings of exclusion (in a place where I'd previously developed my happiness) I needed to refocus my energy into something productive and positive. The space where I'd cultivated happiness suddenly turned into an area where I was discontent and exasperated. A place I for one felt I no longer belonged.

However, what I had nurtured, after several setbacks the previous year, was my spiritual and emotional wellbeing. There was a reason I was focusing on my wellness and this was an opportunity to put into practice everything I had absorbed from the past six months. I decided to redirect my energy, focus, and time into something more lucrative. There was nothing I could do with my current situation, so I asked myself, *In which direction can I focus on learning something new? Where can I invest time in future ideas, projects, and adventures?* I reframed the whole situation. I decided the team member was in fact a diversion, and a reduction of responsibility in my job role meant more time for my personal creativity to thrive. Step by step I placed my efforts into expanding other areas I was good at.

It was then I discovered liberation in the absence of responsibility. The slower pace of work enabled me to open myself up to new projects or opportunities as I searched for something that aligned with my intent and goals for my future. Once I found out what I wanted, I could continue to be successful; I could redirect my energy and push forwards.

From a young girl, I'd dreamed of being in Formula One: that was the goal. I had the vision but for a while I put the dream in the back of my mind whilst creating experiences that enhanced and developed my short-term goals. What I didn't know at the time was everything I was doing would lead to my dream of working in F1 coming true. As I focused on the short-term goals, the long-term one took care of itself. What I knew for sure was I appreciated the challenges life had brought me (even if I didn't see it at the time). Experiencing this challenge while being in motorsport had re-awakened my purpose, my potential, and given me an opportunity to build resilience in order to aim for something more. I reframed these challenges to mean life was presenting me with a series of setbacks because I was being redirected to something that was meant for me.

Stefan Molyneux: *Ladies. You can't be drafted. Sit down when war is discussed.*
Kim Olson, Colonel (retired) – United States Air Force: *A lot of men have told me to 'sit down and shut up' ... Now those men call me Colonel.*

**Setbacks and success**
Many people who encounter setbacks experience feelings of shock, denial, and self-doubt, as well as feelings of rejection. When people do not experience many failures, this frustration can manifest as further upset and anger. Recognising unfortunate events and decisions outside of your control gives you awareness towards ways to move forward. Those defining moments can lead to a series of incidents that can magnify your strengths and in turn allow you to work on any limitations.

Harvard interviewed hundreds of executives who have been fired, laid off, or passed over for a promotion (because of mergers, restructures, competition for top jobs, or personal failings).[1] They concluded that this group went through classic stages of loss, including denial, anger, depression, bargaining, and acceptance (Kübler-Ross model).[2] However, many do not get to the acceptance stage (which I only discovered when researching for this book). Social psychologists found that in decades worth of studies, high achievers usually take considerable credit for their success but assign too much external blame for their failures. Although this protects self-esteem, it prevents learning and growth. Friends and family tend to reinforce this by taking your side and feeding this sense of injustice.

When I decided to speak to my boss directly, he declared he was not able to change the situation nor could he redirect any responsibilities that had been simultaneously promised to both of us. Instead, I was informed that this individual simply had far more experience in management than me. I wasn't even aware this role was being advertised or offered. Though this was a frank and painful realisation it allowed me to accept such changes were beyond my control.

By creating new options within such situations, there are moments where you can turn your loss into a win. Reframing losses as opportunities involves thinking a lot about who you are and what you want. Although escapism is a common reaction – including being busy and avoiding discussing feelings – this rarely leads to a productive transition. Instead,

William Bridges found people would loiter in this twilight zone as they were unable to let go of their current situation and were unclear about what success looked like within their future.[1]

Bickel has championed that resilience promotes career development and success, despite challenges.[3] This correlates with the links I discussed earlier between gratitude and resilience. Furthermore, the role of mentoring and other environmental factors also promotes resilience. Seeking mentors was a great way for me to deliberate future opportunities. It also meant I could reassess where I was and where I wanted to move towards. If you didn't know, one thing I love is a plan, and this gave me the time to discover my 'what' and 'why' regarding my potential as a manager and performance coach. Research by Harvard (supported by career specialist Douglas Hall) showed that although needs and priorities can change over time, perspectives change, and skills may become outdated, so choosing the right opportunity will lead you to the moment when you happen to be looking for one.[1]

The importance of resilience and adaptability is crucial when it comes to career success. However, neither of these qualities come easily. Find ways that can nurture your strengths; identify and develop your limitations; merge them into assets and then these tools can all help navigate you towards your career happiness.

**Weather warning: new storm on the horizon**
That whole year gave me opportunities to seek openings that were in line with my pursuit for happiness. My target was to align with my ultimate career success (despite not knowing exactly what this route entailed). Throughout those months, I continued to challenge myself, took chances to present for new projects, went for job opportunities, and I even attended interviews – all the while staying in a job that made me increasingly unhappy. Despite those risks and potential opportunities, 11 months on I was still there. Five weeks before Christmas (after encountering more disappointments) I decided to put a pin in my active job search and focus on the

present, all the while keeping an eye out for new horizons for the coming year.

It was a fresh Monday morning, and I was in the changing room, post workout, getting ready for a new work week. I knew I was riding a wave of uncertainty in a space filled with unhappiness. I stood in front of the mirror adding the finishing touches to my make-up (my way of putting on a brave face). From the corner of my eye, I noticed my phone ringing. As soon as I clocked the name popping up on the screen, my stomach flipped and my throat became constricted. This was not a scheduled call, which made it highly unusual, and I didn't like the uncertainty it made me feel. The phone call was from a boss who gave me the news I was not expecting: my contract would not be renewed for the following year. Excluding Christmas break, it meant I would have three weeks until I would leave the company and this role.

This unexpected turn left me distraught. I'd done nothing wrong, and I knew it. Despite feeling excluded, I'd managed to work with the responsibilities I'd been given. The aim of my new plan of action was to leave on my terms – but now it was too late and I wasn't ready to leave. My head started to fill up with the pressure of answering questions such as: *What happened?... What do I do now? ... Where do I live? ... How will I make an income?... How do I pay rent in January?* ... Suddenly, I felt the walls around me closing in, the air becoming dense, and I could no longer be in this space. I held it together just in time to escape the environment by taking my bags back to the gym office and offered to do a team coffee run. Thankfully, no one wanted one.

Instead, I took my empty mug as a ruse, grabbed my car keys, and headed straight to my vehicle with full awareness. My car had become my sanctuary during those last few months; it enabled me to feel safe in a workspace where I felt excluded. As thoughts continued to buzz around my head, I felt a sudden loss of control. My emotions had won over and tears began streaming down my cheeks. Despite being unhappy in the role, I began to think about all the friends I'd bonded with, all the support and relationships I'd nurtured and would no longer be around. I was crying because I was leaving a space I once loved, with no idea of which direction to turn or where I would be heading next.

In that moment, I felt like a failure. When I finally got to my car, I sat down, and my breath became short and shallow, I recognised this all too well: I was beginning to have another panic attack. Anxiety and depression had kept me company for such a long time that I was familiar with this stage and its consequences. However, in that horrendous moment, all the work I had done with my spirituality and mindfulness, cultivating my wellbeing from the bounds of countless disappointments, paid off. That was when I heard the voice inside that said,

*Breathe.*
*Just breathe.*

Those three words allowed me to slow down and deepen my breath. Not only did I stop an anxiety attack from coming on; I was able to pause and breathe. With that pause came clarity: I knew I had to be in control of my thoughts and emotions, I knew I could not let this event take me back after coming so far in my personal and emotional journey, even if the news meant I'd le both pain and shock.

Over the previous few years, I had selected a few people I entrusted with my inner demons and turmoil, but this unexpected news threw me back to my old insecurities. My unhappiness had been brewing for some time but had been delayed from resurfacing due to work distractions. That level of anxiety transported me to a place of unknown – that very place where my anxiety and depression stemmed from.

Fortunately, I was given the chance to go home that day and process what had happened. I was surprised to hear it came as a shock to the company management too. However, with my emotions still high, during the journey home I continued to relive the event and possible consequences I would be facing. Suddenly the tears returned and flowed freely. As soon as I walked into the house, I sat down on the sofa without removing my scarf or coat and simply sat there, numb.

That moment was different to any other I had encountered in my past. As if instinctively, I reached out and started to message those I relied on and loved dearly. I was able to connect with those I entrusted and let them know what was going on. I didn't cry for long because I needed to figure out a plan. After an hour of being at home, I reached for my laptop and started searching for jobs: volunteering, anything. As I was searching for jobs and answering friends' messages, I understood: I did not have nor did I need all the answers that day.

I had 15 days left and counting. As the days passed by there was inevitable further disconnect with the rest of the team. I had not been given much compassion or sympathy for the situation I was in as everyone else's contract was secure. That was the moment I knew this was the right call and the right direction for me. At first it felt as if I were the last to know but then I decided this would not be the approach I'd end up taking; I knew I needed to keep my head up and find answers.

Unfortunately – despite what we try and tell ourselves – the body has a natural response to stress. Still coming to terms with the unknown meant I was anxious, nervous, and stressed. Consequently, the situation also affected my sleep: I would wake up and needed to convince myself to breathe and go back to sleep. Those early hours in the morning were the hardest moments to quieten the pressing thoughts on my mind. Instead, I went back to the drawing board and revisited my breathing techniques and tools for sleep that I had developed over the past two years until I could eventually fall back to sleep.

Many days passed by where I replayed the event in my head. I had to force myself to eat for energy (even when I didn't feel like it) and I broke out in spots. I was experiencing headaches and throbbing, itchy eyes. This was exactly the situation I knew I could not prevent – so I thought. Despite being overwhelmed and out of control of the situation, I knew I needed to deliver my best to those I was in contact with because I have an overwhelming need to represent my best self. I sought to deliver the most professional aspect of myself and attempted to fake it as much as I could. I used my car as my sanctuary all the more during those last few weeks. I would often sit and meditate and return to it whenever I needed a five-minute breather. I would have lunch there by myself and I used it as an escape. There were days when I drove away from work so I could have some space for myself, instead of risking being caught sat in my car by someone who recognised me.

In the end, faking it took its toll and I knew I was tired from the lack of quality sleep each night. Despite trying my best to create a nurturing environment where I felt comfortable, in which I'd developed relationships and created a new home, I reverted to those shy girl characteristics, using my car as the escape. I simply felt more comfortable when I was on my own, so I took quiet space for myself. Those few minutes were crucial for my sanity, and I took them when I could.

There was one distinct moment when I realised faking and keeping busy simply wasn't enough, a few days after receiving the news I got home one afternoon, I checked my emails and broke down crying because I saw my tax bill, which was due in January. I immediately fell back into a state of anxiety and sadness; keeping up appearances at work and then breaking down when I was alone had left me split. I felt lost and did not know what to do. Suddenly, that voice came in my mind again saying, *Breathe*.

All at once, it was as if by magic: the dark cloud disappeared from over my head and had completely evaporated. I stopped crying, almost unexpectedly, because it brought me back to the present. I took a fresh piece of paper and wrote down a financial breakdown for myself and what I needed to do in the coming months, and it worked. This trance brought me back into the present moment, and I used that energy to provide me with a clear outcome. Having that somehow gave me the reassurance I yearned for. I had taken time to journal, it allowed me to come back into the present moment; in those few minutes I was given clarity and reassurance that this moment would pass. I sat reflecting on all I was fearful of and analysing what the worst-case scenarios would be. It became clearer to me there were two prominent issues relating to my state of mind:

1. Fear of the unknown.
2. Fear of losing people I loved.

These were reoccurring insecurities I'd endured since my childhood. Seeing these words written in front of me enabled me to understand the emphasis I had placed upon them for so many years. I caught myself recapping the lesson of a podcast I had heard, which helped me realise those fears are totally opposite to love. I understood that love is open, love is kind, love is affectionate, love is generosity, compassion, and tender. It is the opposite of fear and this is something that suddenly made complete sense to me in this new sense of awareness. If I were to receive something of significance, I would need to extend that to myself before I could extend it to others. To eliminate things I was fearful of I would push them out with love.

During this whole experience I had reverted to my younger self: my silent, introverted side had been hiding away until it came forward to rescue me when I needed personal space. This level of distance from others increased as Christmas drew nearer because I still did not know what I was going to do next. As I craved distance from others, it didn't stop me from bringing my best self during coaching sessions and meetings, or when interacting with others. It was tiring keeping up a façade of happiness, when inside I was torn, melancholy, and desolate. I debated whether I should stick to the original plans to go on the New Year's holiday with friends. Thoughts ricocheted about whether I should volunteer, travel for personal development, or get some work experience. Ideas about finishing this book all served to provide me with a sense of hope and a little direction filled with purpose. These all helped initiate the recovery process after the initial earthquake and the messy aftermath. I had discovered that I could lean on key individuals; this allowed me to trust, love, and be vulnerable, something that took me a long while to embrace. Despite having a lack of control in not knowing what to do, the list of potential ideas provided me with structure and the weight started to lift off my shoulders. I had less need to carry around the stress, anxiety, and heartache. I was no longer required to carry the burden of fear or unhappiness. I simply understood this to be a phase where I was treading water. I needed to settle myself into a space where it was OK to not be OK, and embrace the uncertainty of not knowing exactly what would come next.

This was the quintessence of being still, being in the present, and understanding this would not last forever. I was also coming to terms with accepting the need to hold on to something that no longer served me.

Sebastian Vettel, a four-time Formula One World Champion, was given a surprise himself when the team principal called him to tell him there was no further intention for Vettel to continue with the team.[4] Vettel described this as looking for the right opportunity, allowing things to come together, being aware of the decisions and not wanting to rush making a move before establishing clarity about what he wanted to do. This successful driver also encounters setbacks and rejections – we all do.

Placing this new form of rejection in its place, accepting the unknown and tackling the fear that had followed me around for decades finally allowed me to stand still and be OK with where I was before I moved towards where I was supposed to be.

**Calm after the storm**
When we are caught up in the storm there are whirlwinds of emotions (particularly trauma) that may uncover themselves from our past. What is significant to understand is rejection or missed opportunities can often lead us to the direction we needed to pursue all along. Near misses systematically outperform the narrow wins: it is not about the survival of the fittest.

A study was conducted after two young groups of scientists experienced different outcomes: one group had just missed securing a grant (near miss), while the other had secured their grant (narrow win). Ten years later, researchers found those from the 'losing' group had gone on to have more successful and impactful careers than those who had won the grant.[5] The near miss event resulted in the weaker members leaving the field altogether, while those who remained became better versions of themselves. Performance improvement was causally linked with the near miss event itself.

Another report found respondents identified persistence, tenacity, and perseverance in the face of rejection and criticism as characteristics or qualities that are extremely important to career development and success in academic medicine.[3] Therefore, resilience is an integral component for success. Of course, rejection can be disheartening and discouraging, but you must cultivate a certain level of emotional maturity, reframe the rejection to be more positive, and make revisions where necessary.

## TIME TO CONSIDER

1) **Journaling**
Reflecting on your emotions will enable you to confront them rather than survive with their absence through ignorance.

   Friends are a beautiful gift whom we can lean on for support; just bear in mind their opinions and judgements can lead you down a rabbit hole. This means instead of dealing with the situation, it can often be inflated by their views. It can be helpful to vent, yet this is not the conclusion you need when faced with problems facing your career and income.

   Journaling allows you to connect with your emotional intelligence: use this as a superpower because only you know your story – and your considerate friends tend to take your side anyway. If you seek to vent, ask for support, make it clear what the intention is, otherwise you may suffer more when attempting to overcome a particular situation.

2) **When facing challenges try answering the following questions** (suggested answers are given in italics.)

- What can I do to change this situation? *Seek answers from a superior and be open to listening to what they have to say; drop your defensiveness.*
- What habits can I learn to get the job / promotion next time? *Find courses or skills you need to learn to stand out next time.*
- How can I redirect my energy into something more positive? *Find new ways to bolster your strengths and redefine your limitations.*
- Where can I find positive motivation? *This can be intrapersonal or from another individual.*
- What is the worst thing that can happen? *Figure out what is the worst-case scenario.*

**3) Find a mentor**

Seeking mentors when redirecting your ambitions will benefit you immensely.

Pursue mentors who are in roles you desire, as well as those who are successful and experienced in other areas. Your mentors should be people who have an abundance of knowledge and an extensive career path. Hearing from these individuals will allow you to put your own career path in perspective, particularly when it comes to career dilemmas.

*Challenges will always come. Find the lesson, rise above it, and stay grounded to your purpose. Only then are you raising your attention towards your intentions.*

Tulshi Varsani

# CHAPTER TWELVE: THANK YOU, NEXT

*'Thank you for attending your recent assessment day. After careful consideration, we regret to inform you that we will not be proceeding with your application.'*

Before I received the gut-wrenching news that meant I would leave an industry I loved, there was an interim phase where I had fewer responsibilities within my current role. That lack of accountability enabled me to focus on other things, including applying for a new job. As always (with everything I approach) I put as much (if not more) emphasis on the preparation. I am a person who likes to prepare for battle, to navigate through any eventualities – just in case. What I did not prepare for, was failing the interview. It was not that I felt I was a shoo-in, it was more the confidence I nurtured: I knew the role, I had the stamina, work ethic, and ambition to pursue a new challenge. Plus, I craved it.

Not only did an unsuccessful result come as a surprise, but it had also never happened to me before. I was once turned down for an internship, but in the end that eventually led me to take on a higher position as a performance coach. However, on this occasion, it was the very first time I was not offered a job after an interview. For a time, I believe I became stuck in a loop as I did not expect the answer I was given. I felt disheartened as well as disappointed: the time I'd spent in preparation felt wasted and I needed an alternative strategy.

There were so many questions which raced through my mind. Immediate thoughts ran to, *What did I do wrong?* This question always gives me scope to self-reflect and adjust, so I can try and find ways to improve. However, I soon found myself in unknown territory when I was told I would not be receiving any feedback from the interview. I took umbrage and pursued answers until I received some! This experience left me feeling rejected which was jarring because it was unfamiliar territory. I underestimated this level of rejection and its impact because it had never happened within this context. I came to understand any type of rejection is a disappointment, but I was not sure whether I wanted to cry in frustration, throw things in anger, or scream because I had come to a dead end – it was probably a combination of all three.

Instead, I reached out to a small group of friends whom I'd entrusted with the journey of my application, and sent them a message informing them of the decision. They provided me with the level of reassurance when I could not find it within myself and I was so grateful to be fortunate enough to have a strong network of friends and family surround me.

Every time I encounter disappointment, I force myself to remember this quote which is etched on my skin:

*What is for you, won't go by you*
Unknown

This serves as a reminder that it wasn't about the need to forget the moment; nor was it about trusting everything will work out; it was a belief and faith in knowing when you think you are heading for something there might be a new fork in the road. When this happens, you need to remind yourself that what you thought was a path you so desperately wanted was not meant for you at all. Instead, there is always a better path which will lead you to the place that *is* meant for you. This serves as a reminder to have faith in the unknown. Even if you are uncertain and things seem as if they are not going to plan, trust this pause. Trust the unknown. This is what I needed at the time. I was so used to moving on from one project to another, keeping busy and knowing what is next, that to be in a state of pause, to embrace the unknown was unfamiliar.

This would have to be my new norm. This was a phase I needed to embrace.

While I waited to receive the feedback I was pursuing, I decided to seek the answers I needed. I opened a new tab on the internet browser and searched, 'accepting rejection after a job interview'. I must admit I felt ridiculous seeking answers online but after working so hard on the presentation, the accompanying report, and interview process, I coveted answers from outside sources. I thought there must be others' experiences I could learn from, and it turns out I was right.

The internet can be a wonderful and dangerous place all at the same time. It can be difficult to decipher between truth and lies and to recognise which responses may confirm your bias, which can be taken as useful tools, and can be used as constructive examples. Many of our experiences can lead us into a negative state of mind – especially if we have familiar, unhelpful patterns that are forged into our memory whenever things do not go to plan; this can be related to a trigger which reveals past emotions and or memories. Seeking third-party answers, if you will, meant I could apply others' experiences to my own situation. It was important for me to remember I was not alone in this sort of experience. Even though we like to think of ourselves as unique, many encounters have come long before us and will continue after us. It is essential to remember we can learn from our own mistakes as well as the mistakes of others.

The decision to seek answers online gave me reassurance to accept the outcome and the assurance I needed: to be OK with the unknown. This was a great reminder that rejection happens to everyone and despite the lack of certainty there was an opportunity to learn. It served as a reminder on the wins I had up to that point, such as conquering a fear on giving a presentation and attaining an interview out of hundreds of applicants for a multinational organisation. I needed to convince myself what I had planned was enough and I'd done the best I could do, but I was not what they were looking for. This confirmation led me to believe there was another direction meant for me. All this connects with what I wrote in the previous chapter about resilience. Whichever way you may deal with rejection, the key is to deal with it in a healthy way.

## TIME TO CONSIDER

1) **Move your body**
By participating in any form of physical activity you can begin to change your brain chemistry and trick your physiology into acting better, releasing chemicals which enhance your mood and wellbeing. I'm sure you remember my own experiences in chapter six and seven.

Studies have shown the same areas of the brain are activated whether we experience physical pain or feelings of rejection. Eisenberger et al. showed neural activity in the anterior cingulate and right ventral prefrontal cortex found during the experience of social exclusion was similar to that found during experiences of physical pain.[1] This is one reason why rejection hurts so much: neurologically speaking, your body responds to this in the same way as it would if it had experienced physical pain. Although rejection and being disheartened is part of our nature, you can lessen the pain it causes by moving your body and increasing the endorphins: this will help counteract the imbalance you are experiencing. Despite not feeling like it, movement is the best medicine and a great way to overcome the pain.

2) **Talk it out**
Talking to your partner, a friend, or someone who can offer you their ear to listen – without judgement – can be extremely helpful.

It is important, however, not to dwell on rejection, although it can be difficult to accept if you are not given the opportunity to understand the rationale behind it. Countless studies have demonstrated that even mild rejections can lead to people taking out their aggression on innocent passers-by. There is a strong link between rejection and aggression; the experience of rejection raises strong emotions in some people.

Let your loved ones in. Tell them about this part of your life and allow them to support the process you are going through. They can only begin to understand your hurt and pain if you tell them about it, even if the result is just so they can fathom your request for space.

### 3) Moving on

The sooner you deal with the disappointment the more likely it is you will be able to spot the next opportunity. Of course, it's difficult in the moment to face the reality that not every job you apply for will end the way you hope. This life lesson will allow you to build emotional and mental armour. Instead, you can be open to building resilience, as well as persistence within your frame of mind and future. This allows for another opportunity towards growth and spotting potential breaks.

### 4) Reflect – Pause – Meditate

*Reflect*

Remind yourself compassionately that overanalysing will not be productive. Furthermore, it may also delay the action needed to move forward. Ruminating over the scenario is not the same as asking for feedback and acting on the information given. This can be incorporated into future job searches and interviews. Following your reflections try to answer the following questions:

> ➢ What is it you can do to improve for the next challenge?
> ➢ How can you be fantastic next time?
> ➢ Which attributes or features would you see as non-negotiables when looking for a new role?

*Pause*

Strange as it sounds, the reassuring news is that rejection temporarily lowers your IQ, which means that thinking clearly is not easy. Take advantage of this natural reaction by pausing and allowing yourself to take a moment of rest before taking the next step. Be compassionate towards yourself and your needs before you move the needle forwards.

### *Meditate*
Rejection will naturally initiate negative self-talk, particularly when dissecting the reasons that have led to this particular outcome. Thoughts and emotions are in our control, which is something you explore during meditation. If you are someone who struggles with this or you are new to meditating, then you will find references on meditation to quieten your mental chatter in chapter fourteen, and online.[2]

### 5) Create
Draw up a list reminding yourself how amazing you truly are and list some of your accomplishments you have achieved in the past six months, (include the risk and confidence you took to go for that interview!).

Interviews are a great way for you to recap all your accomplishments and showcase yourself in the best light. This is the best time, therefore, to review achievements and will prove essential to provide yourself with a much-needed boost when feeling low.

### 6) Leave on good terms
It can be difficult to do this depending on your expectation on the opportunity you desired, however, leaving on good terms and leaving open connections with the company or the individual who interviewed you allows you to reinforce a status of professionalism and respect – as well as improve your chances for potential future opportunities. This role may not have been the ideal one, but you are a step closer to the one meant for you.

### Success vs failure?
As mentioned in the previous chapter, a near miss can be a good thing. Not only does it increase resilience, but it solidifies

our understanding that success and failure go hand in hand. Oprah Winfrey was fired from her first job in television. Steven Spielberg was rejected from film school multiple times. Michael Jordan did not make his high school's varsity basketball team.

*Every failure is a step to success. Every detection of what is false directs us towards what is true: every trial exhausts some tempting form of error. Not only so; but scarcely any attempt is entirely a failure; scarcely any theory, the result of steady thought, is altogether false; no tempting form of error is without some latent charm derived from truth.*
W. Whewell

When we take a moment to reflect it can lead us to appreciate how important pervasive failure is. That is to say, it is typical and normal to one's personal and professional life.[3,4] Failure can be seen as a dominant and expected outcome in many specialised, goal-orientated outcomes. Michelle Kwan was the most decorated figure skater in United States of America's history. She described the sport itself as impossible and magical. In learning to figure skate she explained it meant falling over and over and over again. Imagine if at ten years old she'd decided she'd had enough of falling and had given up? There would be no Olympian named Michelle Kwan. The dedication of Michelle and her family to this sport contributed to her success.

*Did you know?* In the pharmaceutical industry, the clinical failure rate for drugs entering phase II testing was reported to be 81% (this was for illustrative compounds entering the clinical testing between 1993–2004).[5]

*Did you know?* In major league (baseball) batters fail to hit a ball 75% of the time.

*Did you know?* Even the most accomplished athletes experience losses, injuries, setbacks, and unmet goals. However, they learn, adapt strategies, and improve to achieve success.

Research and innovation in science require failure: it is taught, nurtured, understood, and it is incorporated. It is a shame we are not taught how to accept and deal with failure in schools. How many times were you embarrassed to bring home a bad grade? This isn't how it should be. There are so many ways we can look at failure to problem-solve, reduce personal egos, and embrace ways to build resilience and perseverance. My personal favourite description of failure is: *An opportunity to see our existence close-up. It is a lens through which we begin to see the flaws in our otherwise perfect and perfectly predictable being.*[3]

It forces us to realise the world does not revolve around us. There is no need to guard it with ignorance. Failure can be exposed by embracing humility and learning what failure has taught us. Yang Wang of Northwestern University states individuals can learn from their mistakes and correct them in the next attempt.[6] Wang explained by constantly iterating rather than starting each attempt from scratch, people fail faster and smarter, thus they improve with each attempt.

*In a world of intense competition, failure is an essential ingredient for success*
Co-author James Evans, professor of sociology at University of Chicago[6]

No matter what you are going through, your experiences shape you. And since you get to choose who it is you want to become, take everything you encounter as an opportunity for redirection into a place meant for you.

*My wisdom to share, I think, is really about not giving up – ever. And I think that's a really important thing, that I just keep going. And all of these minor failures don't faze me. I really just enjoy every day, and I think we just have to. You just can't give up, no matter what ... I think that we can change it by just trying to find a new way. I mean, I think rejection isn't really a rejection, it's just a need to redirect.*
Margaret Cho

# CHAPTER THIRTEEN: THRIVE WITH INTENTION

*In Britain today, more than one million people haven't spoken to anybody in the last five days.*
*The Big Issue*[1]

I wrote this book during the middle of the COVID-19 pandemic. At its height, it brought countless families together through singing in the streets, clapping for health services, creating games through social media, and increasing the use of technology so people could work from home. It also reminded us of how much our health and the emergency services manage – despite the lack of support and equipment. There were countless volunteers who assisted with the demands for testing and preventing the disease from spreading, as well as many who looked after the vulnerable and sick. There were also many who suffered alone, who had to isolate by themselves.

Before this pandemic, the stat above stated the need to reach out to others, to support others, and connect. As the population navigated through enforced time apart from loved ones and company, those who were fortunate to be connected through social media were able to reflect on what it was they wanted, whom they wanted that with, and gain an appreciation for those they had in their life. However, this 'connected' era has both benefits and repercussions: consistent access to knowledge can often lead to information overload. Many felt during the pandemic that we were bombarded with various material and sources of data; more than we needed or could comprehend.

Even though the daily news no longer focuses on the pandemic, it is still important to self-select the content we are engaging in, especially in the way we absorb social media. You may recall in chapter nine I detailed how I chose videos specifically to help me sleep, but I restricted all other forms of online content. Social media has proven to cause unhappiness, leading to people developing other mental health issues such as anxiety or depression: but how has this all evolved? This chapter will investigate ways to be selective with information relating to our health, why this is important, and how it affects our wellbeing, as well as how the information can alter our state of mind and regain control of what we learn and attract.

**Information selection**
The decline in happiness and mental health seems paradoxical according to the world happiness report in 2019.[2] We are living in a world within a time where we are arguably in a much better state than we have been at any other time in our history. Violence, criminal rates, and unemployment rates are low.[‡‡‡‡‡‡] Even during 2022 cost of living crisis, overall the standard of living is increasing, and so you would assume the levels of happiness also would rise with this level of affluence, but it has not. In fact, Americans are far less happy and some explanations such as rising obesity levels and increasing substance abuse can contribute to the levels of unhappiness.

Over the past decade, adolescents have increased their time spent on screen activities.[2] By 2017, the average seventeen to eighteen-year-old spent more than six hours per day on three digital media activities: internet, social media, and texting. A world that has brought us technology allows us to access information 24 hours a day, 7 days a week. This also means it is increasingly difficult to switch off from a constant stream of distraction. Whether this is via social media apps, news coverage, books, radio, podcasts, or television:

---

[‡‡‡‡‡‡] This report was conducted before the COVID-19 pandemic caused unemployment rates to rise.

there is plenty that can trigger anxiety, stress, and/or even the likelihood of becoming increasingly lonely.

Creating boundaries with ourselves on how we invite these streams of data into our lives during our day allows us to take back the control and use our time wisely. It can also increase our levels of health and wellbeing. The average American spends just under three hours on their phones, each day! Our obsession is growing: in 2021 Americans checked their phone 262 times per day; in 2022 it was a staggering 344 times per day – that's a 31% increase![3] In March 2018 more than a third of Generation Z (from a survey of 1,000 individuals) stated they were quitting social media for good as 41% stated social media platforms made them feel sad, anxious, or depressed.[4]

Eight of our hours per day (*in addition* to working hours) are being spent attached to a screen of some sort; this includes choosing to spend your free time scrolling through tweets, images, or videos on various other social media apps. This distraction is something many people welcome and invite into their lives until it eventually becomes habitual. And children model this type of behaviour. A study in the United States of America revealed 51% of teenagers felt their parents were distracted by their phone when having a conversation. The way adolescents socialise is vastly different to previous generations. There is far less time getting together engaging in face-to-face interaction with friends and socialising; instead they are becoming increasingly active online. Several studies found girls who spend five hours or more on social media are far more likely (three times even) to become more depressed than non-users. Those who are heavy internet users are also twice as likely to be unhappy.[2]

Overall, activities that relate to smartphones and digital media are linked to lower levels of happiness, whereas individuals who are not involved with technology are linked to increased levels of happiness. If your business means you are predominantly active online, you should bear in mind this can affect how you work and influence what you are absorbing into your mindset. Consequently, this can mean putting tighter restrictions on yourself to be able to manage your time working and socialising away from technological devices – evidence into this is stated below.

Whatever the circumstances regarding the screen time you are accumulating, the evidence is clear: in 2017 Andy Przybylski (University of Oxford) stated fifteen-year-olds should only spend up to four hours a day on screen time. Any more than this has found a direct correlation in a decrease towards their mental wellbeing.[5] Przybylski suggests a phone curfew for children – typically no phones an hour before bed. However, as adults we excuse ourselves and bypass this same recommendation, in turn compromising our quality of sleep. Head over to chapter nine for the recap and recommendations on what constitutes a healthy bedtime routine to increase quality sleep.

**A healthy mind**
When you wake up each morning, imagine this state of awakening like the morning sunrise. You are surfacing from a deep sleep state and although you may be rested, you may also be a little sleepy. Within this moment, you have little to no mental chatter and you are in a space that is intimate and open. If you find yourself having a random thought, you have already missed that moment. It is why monks rise early and meditate immediately: the best moment to meditate is during this semi-conscious state before the restless (monkey) mind kicks in and you have your first of 60,000–80,000 repetitive thoughts that day. The moment you awake, your brain is very receptive to influence because the mind takes shape of whatever it rests upon.

*The mind is everything.*
*What you think, you become.*
Buddha

Your morning routine will enable you to have a mindset which will set you up for the rest of your day. Many successful people, who accomplish far more in their day, begin by setting a clear intention. Some regularly write down exactly what they wish to achieve during their day. Let me be clear, this is not a to-do list; it's an intention of attitude, willingness to learn, and (in some cases) a chance to allow gratitude into your day. Purposeful intention setting allows you to be in the driving seat and predict which direction you wish to take, each and every morning. Having an intention sets accountability and the very act of setting intentions means you begin to make them a priority. This is the polar opposite to allowing whatever the day brings and having scattered attention. By purposefully setting yourself up for the day you are intentionally building focus and bringing awareness towards your day, thus creating success in a particular direction of your choice. By adopting this method, you are prioritising what you wish to accomplish and will therefore navigate your day towards those opportunities and goals.

Setting an intention also means you are more receptive and open to new opportunities. You are declaring your will to see and listen out for all the possibilities around you and your goals. For example, if you should set an intention to train first thing in the day, you are building the habit of performing physical activity for your body, nurturing goals which focus on your strength, flexibility, and/or fitness. In return you will be given access to more focus and energy throughout your day.

Additionally, by setting an intention to reserve some quiet time for yourself, you are creating boundaries and prioritising mindfulness. This could include doing something you enjoy such as listening to a podcast, walking outdoors, or reading a book. This intention allows you to sustain a level of health for your mindset, leading you to feel an increased level of happiness and therefore having more energy for others in your reserves.

There is no clear evidence of this, but Tristan Harris, former Google design ethicist[§§§§§§] suggests looking at our phone first thing in the morning frames your experiences. If you place focus on what you have missed the day before, that is where your attention will remain and it will continue in this

---

[§§§§§§] A design ethicist is someone who evaluates the moral implications of design decisions and takes responsibility for the effect those decisions have on the world at large.

manner throughout your day. Morning routines of the most successful and productive people omit phone use first thing in the morning.

*Neurons fire together, wire together.*
Donald Hebb

Your brain has two states: reactive and responsive. Once your basic needs are met, your brain defaults to a responsive mode. You are safe, relaxed, calm, and at peace. In the responsive mode you are likely to experience more feelings of gratitude, joy, contentment, intimacy, kindness, and compassion. Spending time in a responsive state strengthens our neural substrates. In the responsive mode, though you are more likely to meet challenges, they are not likely to become stressors. Your brain essentially prevents these things from disturbing your peace; you can deal with such things deemed to be a 'threat' but have no regard for fear, frustration, or heartache. Therefore, the more time you spend in this responsive state, the more your brain strengthens these neurological signals to the rest of your body.

In other words, your central nervous system underlies a specific behaviour, cognitive process, or psychological state. Upon waking, your brain is like a sponge; it will absorb everything that requires your focus and immediate attention. By focusing on a daily intention of what you would like to do, you are rewiring and strengthening the neurons that encourage this responsive state. When setting intentions of how the day is likely to go or if you envision what you would like to achieve in the day, you are already setting yourself up with the intention for success.

I have a dear friend of mine who takes the opportunity every morning to write down three things she wishes to accomplish during her day. They also must fit onto the tiniest of Post-it notes. She takes this note and places it in her wallet. Then, as the day continues, it provides a reminder of her intentions, which are uniquely specific to her goals, values, or her character. She often writes them to help navigate herself through times of chaos during her workday. Some intentions may include a coffee with a friend, calling a loved one, or spending time on a particular project.

By setting aside a moment to establish intentions for the day, you are making them manageable habits and digestible goals for the short term, some of which will develop your long-term ambitions – such as creativity and focus with areas including your professional or physical goals. The intentions you choose will enable your health and wellbeing to thrive, consistently. Writing things in a quiet space (from within a responsive state) allows you to nourish a concept into a realistic target. The most important thing that can be oversighted is to understand what you would like to do for yourself: how can you create a better version of yourself or the version you aspire to be? This version can also mean giving the best part of you to others, particularly your loved ones.

Be conscious of the difference between an intention and a to-do list. Intention setting does not need to include any more than three intentions: it should feel manageable, achievable, and motivational. To start, you may feel these intentions will include a list of what you are able to do for yourself, such as carving space for your mental health, breathing, or reading a book.

**Healthy body**
Poor emotional health can weaken your immune system leading to colds, infections, or even substance abuse, as well as rewire the brain, leaving a person vulnerable to anxiety and depression. Chronic stress from negative feelings of hopelessness and helplessness can upset the body's hormonal balance. Consequently, this depletes the brain's chemicals that are needed to feel happy.

When we focus on the positive aspects of our lives, we demonstrate awe and gratitude and strengthen the thoughts that alleviate many symptoms caused by emotional health triggers. Research has presented findings that meditation practices, positive imaging, and muscle relaxation techniques are all instrumental when attempting to alleviate symptoms of poor health. Learning becomes effective when it is enjoyed.

The release of dopamine transmits feelings of enjoyment: when we can do something that teaches us new information – particularly if we move our body at the same time – we are encouraging the levels of dopamine to increase. This could include a new training routine: the more consistent you are, the better you become, and therefore you will most likely enjoy it more as your competency increases. This pattern encourages the cycle to continue until you can see the long-term benefits of your consistent training.

There were days when I knew I was feeling very emotionally vulnerable, often experiencing feelings of dejection with life, my job, and where I was heading (particularly during the later phases of my role). My friends managed to intervene before I suffered a full-blown burnout; something that was oblivious to me was recognised by them in the way I carried myself. It was then I was instructed, quite harshly, to take care of my wellbeing and to change my attitude about my own health and professional habits. The thing that served me was a gentle yoga practice called Yin Yoga. This is a very slow-paced type of yoga, which focuses on quietening the mind and staying in poses for greater lengths of time.

Up until that point, my training had always been systematic and regularly completed in a gym. Although I felt physically and mentally exhausted, I knew I still needed to exercise because it would enhance my mental and physical wellbeing. However, I couldn't muster up the energy to train with the intensity I used to when I was full of motivation and energy. So I found an alternative exercise regime. This gentle yoga sequence was perfect for that phase of my life, when I was feeling lost, unsure, and out of control. It raised my levels of comfort and security, and it was something I could do within the solace of my own home. I used this resource to guide me out of my exhausted phase; it allowed me to be more compassionate, gentle, and loving to myself. It allowed me to sit quietly with my thoughts and be uncomfortable in a safe space, in the absence of distractions. I felt my energy levels replenished and my mental state found space that harboured newfound clarity, that became my intention. This made it easier to integrate my yoga routine with my regular weight training programme.

This new pattern of training extended the responsive mode my brain was in. Moving and stretching first thing in the morning was different to working out in the gym; I felt more focused within the present moment. Yoga was an avenue I could use when I arose in the morning after a restless night's sleep. Movement increases the levels of serotonin and dopamine, so practising my gentle yoga routine while in my responsive state helped strengthen those neural pathways.

Another habit I adopted was refusing to look at my phone until I left for work. This kept me in my own wellbeing bubble, away from the outside world, and it greatly enhanced my mental health. What I found to be the most beneficial outcome was the overall reduction in mental chatter. That new routine directed me to focus on my body and create a healthier version of myself. Most importantly, it equipped me with the ability to sustain some degree of cultivating my responsive brain. Purposefully *not* looking at my phone allowed me to become more selective regarding what I chose to absorb first thing in the morning. This morning routine enhanced the probability of a healthy body, a healthy mindset, and an attitude of positivity regarding my day. Movement was already one of my daily intentions and swapping the habit of being distracted by my phone meant I could absorb and integrate gentle movement before I got to work.

One of the most significant differences was an increase in mental clarity: I felt more assured in overcoming any challenges that may crop up in a personal or work situation. It gave me awareness in observing my attitude, behaviour, and emotions. Previously, I would linger on a negative situation or ruminate over it for hours and days after. However, my practice served me during daily life because I began to observe unplanned events as standalone. My morning routine allowed me to cultivate how to live in the present moment by developing my neurological responses. Prioritising stimulating movement for my physical health gave me access to intentionally flourish my state of mind.

Become mindful of your thoughts when you first wake up. If you pick your phone up while you are still in your responsive mode, you are inviting distractions and society's narratives into your morning and day ahead. By using your phone before tuning into yourself, you are more likely to ignore what you are thinking and feeling, and this is an important gateway towards understanding why you feel and act the way you do now. By using media, you mute your body's reactions and prevent yourself from understanding the deeper meaning of how you feel and why. In previous chapters I mentioned how I had been neglecting my gut feeling. It is important to be aware of the signs and signals your body is giving you as it is your body's version of morse code.

**Healthy attitude**
Whether you naturally see a glass as half full or half empty, there are ways to encourage your mind to develop a healthier attitude, such as: limiting your time on social media or selecting things that will nurture a healthy state of mind and attitude; gaining a positive attitude so you can envision a good outcome (despite any seemingly negative or challenging situations); and reframing your attitude into thinking positively.

All these conscious changes will alter and affect your approach, particularly when you assess and absorb things happening in your daily life. These benefits include anticipating happiness, health, success, and greeting opportunities because you are simply more aware of them when they surface.

Before I got into weight training, I would run. For miles. I loved the way no one else would be up. The world would be quiet and still and all I had was my feet pounding the concrete whilst music blared in my ears. Until I couldn't do it anymore. I hurt myself, badly. Being a coach and someone who avoids the doctor, I figured it wasn't all that serious and I could manage my own recovery. But years after my 'recovery', aches and pains would crop up around my hip (back then I didn't understand I was harbouring muscle weakness and emotional trauma). It became uncomfortable when I would sit for long periods of time; I would fidget a lot or find my knee injury would flare up from time to time, despite having stopped running.

Years later, when I was practising meditation consistently, the injury cropped up again. This time, I decided to try something different. I attempted to use a visualisation technique, filled with love and self-compassion to navigate healing towards those two areas that caused me so much pain. I figured, what is the harm in visualising my body into a healthier state? I concluded there wasn't any harm in trying, so tried it just the once.

I didn't notice anything drastically different until I'd been talking to a friend during the coronavirus pandemic, when I paused. We had been on the phone for almost 90 minutes. I'd been sitting in the most awkward position on the sofa, and I hadn't moved. I also hadn't felt any pain around my back or hip area. This revelation was like magic.

By that point, I'd been suffering with that pain for almost ten years. I'd done lots of strength, rehab, and recovery sessions; the visualisation method was the only thing I'd done differently. I'd set an intention during a meditation practice to heal that part of my body: I'd visualised it healing, and it had worked. For some time after, I felt it was too good to be true – like when you've had hiccups for a while and when they leave you still expect them to continue. The inspiration came from Dr Joe Dispenza, but I conducted my own application and sequence. I have since tried it on other areas of my body and realised the power of intention setting and meditation means I can heal.

When you are bombarded with information you deny yourself the opportunity to decode what your body is trying to tell you: that requires silence. Delaying checking social media or watching the news can allow you to be mindful of recurring patterns of behaviour, helping you identify what is good, positive, unpleasant, or negative. It can also be useful to simply observe things around you without judgement. During this time, you are given the opportunity to take stock of what you are feeling, what tensions you are holding on to within your body, as well as what barriers are holding you back. Your body has the answer: you just need to make an intention to listen to what it's telling you. This self-assessment will allow you to decipher between what you like about your current state and which elements you can change to benefit your overall levels of happiness and success. This analysis will enable you to reflect on your current relationships, work life, or happiness and success in general. You may also find it enhances your interpretation when it comes to your own feelings, triggers or resistance to things that are not serving you and ways you can heighten your own wellbeing through nutrition, sleep, and movement.

By accepting our shortcomings, we are better able to understand the ways we are self-sabotaging and remaining within a state of fixed mindset versus a growth mindset. Bombarding ourselves with information rewires our attitude and can cause us to feel like we are losing control, when really we have been leading our attention and intention in a direction that causes us further stress, anxiety as well as increasing uncertainty. There are ways to reverse this.

My intention setting evolved into placing topics for the day ahead, which I've detailed below. Such questions allowed me to focus on the importance of nurturing my health, wellbeing, relationships, and business. It was a way to create non-negotiables in my day, to create healthier habits, and made me accountable at the end of the day. Feel free to take the following examples as ideas for intentions to set yourself.

## TIME TO CONSIDER

1. **What can I do for my mind?**
   I set an intention which included meditation. This was to cultivate my personal aim to practise on a more consistent basis because I felt the benefits throughout my day. These benefits scaled up in the weeks and months that followed consistent practice.

   Other intentions included reading before bedtime. This helped increase the absence of social media before I slept and encouraged me to get through the books I so often neglected to read.

2. **What can I do for my body?**
Physical exercise is such a large part of my life: not only is it ingrained in my career as a performance coach, but I use this to nurture my physical wellbeing and mental health (as detailed in chapter seven) by adopting a new practise that maintained my responsive mindset in the mornings. By refocusing my energy towards my goals, I was able to create a morning routine that served me physically, mentally, and spiritually. I found myself getting stronger, fitter, and healthier. Additionally, practising presence during the flow within the training session allowed me to enjoy the time spent in my element pushing myself both mentally and physically.

3. **What can I do for my soul?**
Again, meditation is something I focused on for this area in my life. It provided a way to reconnect to a quiet space. The aim was to quieten the mental chatter, and I found it reduced my levels of anxiety. However, I do not rely solely on meditation for this sense of relief. I find talking to a friend can also help lift my spirits, whether I'm feeling low or joyous. I enjoy frequently connecting to particular people because it feeds my soul. Writing an intention to meet someone for a coffee could be the soulful connection you need but you keep putting off because 'life gets in the way'.

These are a few examples which you may take and apply to your lifestyle. Create something unique and important to *you* as it needs to stem from what your purpose is and why. The possibilities can match your intentions of who you are now and what you want to nurture to benefit you in the future. These are hard questions to answer. If you find you are struggling, look back on previous chapters so you can come to this conclusion with a little more ease. When you place an intention, it may mean dedicating space and time towards something you want to energise, as well as emphasising your goals and needs. It may include cultivating relationships, personal growth, or learning a new skill before it becomes a habit. With time, you will be able to answer questions such as:

- ➢ What can I do for myself?
- ➢ What can I do for my partner?
- ➢ What can I do for a stranger?

## CHAPTER FOURTEEN: ZEN AS FU*K

*Practising meditation is a ritual that will cultivate your creativity to design your dream life and open dimensions that unleash a source of unlimited possibilities.*
Tulshi Varsani

I would describe meditation as splitting me into two mindsets which I can only describe (perhaps simplistically) as a positive and negative state. The first state gives me a strong sense of comfort and joy; true moments of Zen.******* These experiences give me a renewed sense of energy and an increased state of flow. I recall moments where I slipped into what seemed like another realm, a gap between when you are about to enter the stage of sleep and before the moment you experience a dream state. No thoughts, just stillness. It was as though I'd entered a void, where there was no time, no noise, no comprehension of existence, and where nothing else mattered. It was where my body and mind were relaxed, and I reached complete stillness. Even moments after waking from this state, I carried this positive cloud around with me throughout my day. Residual effects included encountering moments of rejuvenation and feeling contentment – as if my

---

******* Zen is a school of Mahayana Buddhism that originated in China during the Tang dynasty. It emphasises the use of meditation and direct, intuitive insight into one's true nature, rather than having reliance on religious texts or rituals. Zen teachings stress importance on attainting a state of 'no-mind', where the mind is free from thoughts and distractions, where one is able to see things as they truly are.

resources had been topped up. I felt complete, with a new sense of reassurance and self-confidence.

The second mindset I experienced from meditation left me with inner conflict, experiencing feelings of struggle, frustration, and sometimes anxiety. Once I had the sense of what meditation *should* be (as I experienced it above), when that did not happen as frequently as I anticipated (i.e. every time I meditate) I was left defeated and under the impression my meditation practice had not been fulfilled nor accomplished. These days, however, I am aware that my preconceived ideas stem from my interpretation of what *should* happen, as well as comparing it to previous encounters. When I compared such positive meditative experiences with the times when I did not feel stillness or experience that sense of tranquillity, this led me to believe I'd encountered a poor practice.

Furthermore, arriving to a point where I even wanted to meditate came from a place of severe unrest. The practice itself took time and I allowed myself to try out several different approaches to meditation – I share this experience with you later in this chapter.

At times I would be enthralled by my mental chatter. Thoughts and ideas would swim around my head which meant the whole ritual would be a constant cycle of repetitiveness, practising 'stillness', and refocusing my attention. I admit, there were plenty of times where I would allow thoughts to distract and entice me into a world of imagination and I would often allow my thoughts to stray into previous memories and visualise future situations.

Now I understand *both* experiences of my meditation practice enabled me to learn what was really going on in my head and heart. I understood how they enhanced my knowledge and awareness around triggers, emotions, and focus. I was able to sift through specific (previously hidden) emotions and uncover feelings I wasn't aware existed. Meditation provided me with an opportunity to delve deeper into my past and remain grounded in the present. It gave me tools to be still and practise patience, emphasise self-compassion, encounter forgiveness, as well as open many opportunities for personal growth. It encouraged expansion into discovering new depths of who I am, about the world around me, and the ways I'd held on to previous trauma. Meditation has given me many things including a chance to regain focus and bring attention to the present, allowing me to accept the beauty within the now. I acknowledged how discovering both difficulties and bliss within meditation led me towards the journey of evolving. It was to evolve beyond the hurt in life, put to rest the trauma experienced, change the fears I anticipated, and merge into the person I wanted to become.

What I knew for sure, particularly when experiencing difficult moments in meditative practices, is that none of us are the same person we were yesterday, last week, last month, or the year before. We are constantly learning, engaging, and finding new ways to enrich our experiences here on Earth. If we are fully present, each moment can sink us into a deeper understanding of that topic we are studying, connecting us deeply with the person we are engaging with, and figuring out ways to sustain a happier life. Therefore, meditation has taught me (and continues to teach me) that no matter what the day, time, or which method I will use, the practice is always new, every time. It can also be imperfect, but this is a part of the process; this is a part of my process.

If we allow ourselves to practise as if we are learning, it encourages us to release any expectations, accept the current state, and recognise the reality of what 'is'. My revised attitude towards meditation allows me to comprehend that each practise is a new experience. More than that: it is an opportunity to learn something new.

Let's use food as an example to give you an alternative perspective on what I mean. None of us would say to ourselves, 'We will neither eat nor drink anything for the rest of the week because yesterday we gorged on a large meal.' We understand there is balance in each day, we accumulate the energy required for that day alone. If we take meditation as a similar way to digest this, we can enable meditation to serve us each day because it serves our present focus and taps into more resources needed. When we are able to top up our energy needs for the day, we consistently eat well day after day, and eventually we create a body that serves us energetically throughout our existence, no matter what circumstances we face. We are healthy, fit, and able to fight off disease because we are building our immune system for the long term. This is similar to how meditation benefits you in both the short and long term. The realisation for me was that meditation gave me the sense of being better than I was and so I lowered the expectations I placed on each practice.

If we adapt our thinking from wanting perfection and instead start from zero when the new day begins, we can establish a stronger connection within ourselves and our practice. Having battled with trying to perfect my practice, this 'start from zero' methodology allowed me to be more compassionate and trust the journey which was ever expansive. Not only had my interpretation merged into raising awareness of the benefits within meditation, it also enabled me to crave the need to understand the science behind the practice, as well as its effects on the body.

Meditation was once considered an exclusively Eastern practice; it was (and to some degree still is) associated with religion or spirituality. Luckily for us, studies worldwide are supporting its relevance to any person's overall health and wellbeing, and meditation is adopted by many successful and happier individuals. Before I expand on that, I want to share the depths and origins of meditation, as well as extracting the science behind what meditation does to the body's biology and the effect it has on us. I had been practising meditation for a few years before I decided to find out more about its history. What I discovered provided both fascination with and motivation for continuing with my meditative practice. Many people can be discouraged from meditating because of their own preconceived notions and ideas – perhaps their experiences thus far haven't been so fruitful. This chapter will be useful for those who prefer empirical evidence, as it provides the scientific analyses regarding the benefits of meditation. It is also aimed to give you an opportunity to try again with something that will work for you, your wellbeing, and overall happiness. Above all, there are many reasons why meditation is so fruitful.

*Meditation and yoga are a marriage; they sync with one another.*
*When you bring your mediation onto the (yoga) mat you raise your vibration as you practise movement.*
*What you cultivate on the mat will be visible once you encounter hardships off the mat.*
*Your perspective of what is classed as hardship will change.*
*Your mindset will shift your response to the way you manage difficulties.*
*This is what mediation does: it can be felt, done, practised anywhere, at any time.*

Tulshi Varsani

**Origins of meditation**
The term 'meditate' was introduced in the twelfth century AD, from the Latin *meditatus* 'to think or reflect upon', but the actual practice of meditation goes back thousands of years. Buddha (origin, India) was a prince who became a monk, philosopher, and leader. Buddhism was founded on his teachings. Buddhist texts refer to many different practices of meditation as Buddha sought enlightenment and ways to enhance self-fulfilment. Closely attached to Buddhism, meditation is referred to be bhāvanā,[††††††] which is achieved through different techniques such as mindfulness, concentration, loving kindness, etc; or dhyāna,[‡‡‡‡‡‡] which is key for developing mindfulness and insight, with the ability to see things as they are.[1]

---

[††††††] Also spelt 'bhavana', it means 'cultivation' or 'development'. In Buddhism, bhavana refers to the practice of mental cultivation or the development of the mind through meditation. The goal of bhavana is to cultivate positive qualities such as compassion and to purify the mind, as well as to ultimately achieve the state of enlightenment.
[‡‡‡‡‡‡] Also spelt 'dhyana' or 'jhana', this is a term from Buddhism and Hinduism referring to a state of mind, deep concentration or meditation. Dhyana is one of the eight elements of the Eightfold Path, considered to be prerequisite for achieving the state of enlightenment.

Evidence of meditation practice dates back thousands of years; at least the first millennium BCE. Earliest documented records mention meditation around 1500 BCE from Hindu traditions of Vendatism. However, it is now commonly believed that neighbouring countries China and Japan developed practices even earlier than this; around the fifth century BCE. (Though historians still debate where these origins have come from). Lao-Tze (also rendered as Laozi and Lao Tzu) was a Chinese philosopher and author of *Tao Te Ching*, in which he exemplifies his thoughts and teachings, referencing meditation.

Dōshō was a Japanese monk in the first century AD who travelled to China to study Buddhism. He learnt the process of Zen and created a community of monks teaching zazen, a form of seated meditation in Japan.[1] Throughout the Middle Ages, meditation practices grew into religious traditions as a form of prayer.

During the 1700s the West began to adopt meditation founded from Eastern philosophy. Texts containing references to meditation from India were translated into various European languages including the *Upanishads*, the *Bhagavad Gita*, and the *Buddhist Sutras*. In the eighteenth century Voltaire wrote discursive texts on meditation, followed by Schopenhauer in the nineteenth century. Swami Vivekananda brought meditation to prominence in the United States of America after speaking in Chicago in 1893.

From this point, Eastern models of spirituality experienced an evolving surge within Western culture. After its introduction to the West, meditation was progressively removed from religious connections and teachings. The 1960s and 1970s brought increasing investment into researching its practices, which resulted in detaching meditation further from spiritual fulfilment. Even pop culture celebrities like The Beatles practised Transcendental Meditation®. *The Relaxation Response* by Herbert Benson in 1975 explored meditation on mental and physiological outcomes.[2] By the late 1970s, Professor Jon Kabat-Zinn began investigating health benefits of meditative practice and later introduced the 'mindful-based stress reduction' (MBSR) programme, included in his Mindfulness Stress Reduction Clinic.[3] Another spiritual practitioner and doctor, Deepak Chopra, featured on Oprah in 1996 with his book *Ageless Body, Timeless Mind* and mediation soon became a celebrity endorsed practice. The concept of 'mindfulness' was evolving, as was the approach in cognitive behavioural therapy (CBT).

**Neurological evidence and meditation**
Once the West began to understand the benefits of meditation, more scientific research was conducted to explain how the human body responds to this type of activity. Research dating as far back as 1936 started to evidence meditation within the field of psychology. An electroencephalogram (EEG) (which records electrical waves of brain activity) was included in research involving a yogi, Swami Rama. American psychologists investigated the control Swami Rama had over his bodily functions, once thought to be involuntary. Swami Rama demonstrated the ability to produce different types of brain waves – such as alpha, beta, theta, and delta – on demand. The ability to alter his heartbeat radically – from beating at 300 beats per minute to stopping it for a few seconds – were also recorded. This yogi even had the ability to remain conscious whilst his brain was in the deep sleep cycle. He was even able to demonstrate the ability to control his skin and internal body temperature.[4]

From a biochemical point of view, we are aware that stress is shown to predispose chronic sufferers to developing diseases such as heart attack, cancer, and infections to name a few. Neurotransmitters play a key role in modulating and regulating behaviour and anxiety. One neurotransmitter is gamma-aminobutyric acid (GABA), a chemical messenger in the brain that helps regulate brain activity. It inhibits activities of other neurons and balances the effects of excitatory neurotransmitters. Low levels of this neurotransmitter have been linked to anxiety and epilepsy.

Positron emission tomography (PET) scans are used to produce detailed three-dimensional images of the inside of the body. They highlight any abnormal areas and how well certain functions of the body are working. When PET was used to compare the regional cerebral blood flow (rCBF) of eight Tibetan Buddhist meditators whilst they performed complex cognitive tasks, they presented with significantly higher rCBF in the prefrontal cortex than the control group; this part of the brain is largely responsible for executive functions such as decision-making and problem-solving. Higher levels of rCBF stimulate and activate the reticular nucleus of the thalamus, that in turn increases production of GABA. Another large-scale study found regularly meditating decreases the likelihood of developing depression and other mood-related disorders.[5]

Deficiency in serotonin (a neurotransmitter which plays a key role in mood regulation, see footnote on p.109) is associated with depression. An experiment was conducted (using PET scan) where serotonin levels in healthy controls were compared with patients diagnosed with panic disorder. It found that patients diagnosed with panic disorder had one-third lower levels of serotonin 1A receptors in the anterior cingulate, posterior cingulate, and midbrain raphe (associated with emotion, social behaviour, and attention).[6] Several other studies performed on individuals concluded meditation practices (whilst observing urinal excretion) increased the breakdown products such as serotonin in the urine. Transcendental Meditation® practitioners exhibited higher levels of serotonin compared with the control group (who didn't meditate) and much higher levels post meditation.

**Meditation and health**
Transcendental Meditation® involves repetition of a sound (called a mantra) for 15–20 minutes, at least twice a day. The individual experiences a state of relaxational awareness. Clinical trials by Anderson found regular Transcendental Meditation® may have the potential to reduce systolic and diastolic blood pressure by approximately 4.7 and 3.2mmHg, respectively.[7] Rainforth conducted a meta-analysis of 17 trials (a total of 960 participants) of patients with elevated blood pressure and found evidence which indicated, among stress reduction approaches, a Transcendental Meditation®

programme is associated with significant reductions in blood pressure.[8]

EEG recordings were conducted on voluntary participants before and after three months of meditation training. Fast Fourier transform (FFT) and Endler Multidimensional Anxiety Scales (EMAS) were used to measure the coherence levels in alpha, beta, theta, and delta frequency bands. Changes in EEG patterns after meditation practice were found mostly within the theta frequency. The theta power decreased on the left but not the right hemisphere of the brain. This was similar to the findings for the delta frequency. The beta frequency decreased states of anxiety and cognitive worry. The research concluded that the left hemisphere of the brain is more sensitive to meditation practice and significant in treating disorders such as anxiety.[9]

Another review which examined clinical trials on complementary approaches found that a variety of sources – including acupuncture, yoga, tai chi, massage therapy, and relaxation techniques – all had more positive than negative results. The trials found such complementary approaches helped patients in conditions which eased back pain, osteoarthritis in the knee, neck pain, severe headaches, and migraines. Physical diseases and ailments including gastrointestinal were used to study the effects of stress in the body. After completing the IBS severity scale, 75 women were assigned to an eight-week mindfulness programme. They completed a quality of life and mindfulness questionnaire before and after the initiative. Results demonstrated mindfulness training had a substantial therapeutic effect in bowel symptom severity, quality of life, and reduction in stress.[10]

**Meditation and cognitive function**
There is a growing body of research on the effects of meditation on cognitive function. Some studies have found regular meditation practices can improve attention, memory, and executive function, as well as reducing stress and anxiety – as mentioned earlier. One study in the journal *Frontiers in Human Neuroscience* found that an eight-week mindfulness

meditation programme improved participants' ability to sustain attention and working memory, as well as reduced symptoms of anxiety and depression.[11]

Brain researchers Dr Fred Travis and Dr Yvonne Lagrosen investigated why some people are always alert, interested in learning new things, and disposed to seeing the whole picture.[12] Their study worked with 21 product engineers, who – when initially tested – were found to have above average results for creativity and successful problem-solving. Attaching these individuals to an EEG device, they were tested on swiftness of decision-making, speed of processing information, and sense of coherence. This data was used to identify and quantify brain integration, found to be higher amongst those who scored better on creativity tests. For some, creativity is the key to reaching that state of mindfulness. Dr Lagrosen highlighted that creativity, in the form of flexibility and originality, is connected to the whole brain functioning.

Previous research studies by Rubik found inner experiences associated with increased clarified gamma amplitude from the prefrontal cortex involves positive emotions of happiness and love, along with reduced stress.[13] Transcendental Meditation® practitioners achieved greater increases in gamma frequency from the prefrontal region over controls during neurofeedback sessions. Dr Travis explains people who wish to excel in any field should consider learning Transcendental Meditation®; they will be able to see for themselves the effect of regular transcending on inner happiness and outer success.

A study was conducted on middle school students in the United States of America which involved 189 students who were below proficiency level at baseline in English and maths – evaluated on California Standards Tests and compared to controls.[14] Out of the 189 students in the study, 97% were racial and ethnic minority students and the Transcendental Meditation® Program was part of the school's programme for three months. Before completing their final test, the results indicated improvements for students who meditated, in comparison to the control group. A greater percentage of students improved at least one performance level in English and maths. This study implies that at-risk students who practise Transcendental Meditation® can improve academically, subsequently closing the achievement gap. Another study on an eight-week mindful meditation course found people who are regular practitioners had a heightened attention and concentration span. Participants who meditated demonstrated more focus, in comparison to those who did not.[15]

It is worth noting research on meditation and cognitive function is still in its early stages and more research is needed to fully understand the relationship between meditation and cognitive function, as well as how different types of meditation may affect cognitive function differently.

**Relationships and meditation**
A psychological study reported on 17 married women who received instruction for a Transcendental Meditation® programme – but they did not know that it was related to meditation.[16] The group subjects, who practised regularly, showed significantly greater marital satisfaction than controls who were not practising. Relationships were enhanced due to mindfulness interventions, and the couples' levels of relationship satisfaction, autonomy, relatedness, closeness, and acceptance of one another were particularly beneficial for couples who practised mindfulness. It led to improving relationship happiness and managing relationship stress.[16]

Meditation practices provide a pathway for individuals to experience relational connection in themselves and with others. This relational perspective invites understanding and accountability in terms of sensitivities and responding to the moment-to-moment interactions. A mindfulness-based practice that combines loving kindness can also open activities and relationships to be fresh, pristine, and miraculous.[17]

## Meditation and me

As research has emphasised, meditation enhances empathy, cognition, and it is a natural stress stabiliser. It also promotes individuals' overall health and wellbeing, and increases emotional health via positive thinking. My reconnection with mediation occurred once I'd reached a point where I was nearing physical and mental exhaustion. I believe I was a few steps away from burning out: work was demanding more of my attention and time; my lack of boundaries meant I would succumb to increasing my workload, without consideration for my personal health and wellbeing.

This type of exhaustion was noticeable when I experienced significant dips in my concentration. I lacked focus and experienced significant restlessness within my sleeping patterns. I was conscious how this type of fatigue led not only to cognitive decline, but also to poor nutritional choices. My mindless behaviour resulted in me reaching for sugary foods or caffeine to keep me engaged and alert. This was a clear indicator that I was physically and emotionally drained; I was constantly adding sugar to my diet to top up my energy levels.

My wakeup call from my friends alerted me to an intuition I had been ignoring and I felt drawn to practise yoga and meditation, via Yin Yoga. My sole purpose was to sit quietly and attempt to ease my racing thoughts, particularly when I needed to sleep and stay asleep throughout the night. I craved the need to ease my internal chatter, which was keeping me from sleeping and remaining asleep. This constant mental babble had led to greater degrees of anxiety and stress, so this meditation practice was purposeful action towards reducing the mental chatter.

My personal exploration of meditation was a journey to determine which practices best suited me, which evolved and changed as I progressed through my spiritual voyage. Sitting quietly often did not work, especially during the initial stages of reconnecting with meditation. This meant I required an increasing amount of support from practices that incorporated guided stories. Once I had begun to master such techniques, I added affirmations, incorporated breath work, and recited mantras. As I grew my knowledge and stamina within these areas, they served their purpose along my journey and practices.

Meditation quietened my internal chatter; the very thing I needed. It consequently allowed me to sleep better, which then enabled me to regain energy in key areas of my life. What I didn't expect was additional benefits such as increasing my level of focus, concentration, and creativity. I was a happier and more positive person, and I used that energy to put good food into my body again and become more mindful of what I was consuming daily. It also enabled me to put extra energy into my training. Overall, it provided access into an area within me that cultivated stillness and increased my sense of contentment. I didn't expect to gain any of these additional benefits from mediation, but I figure it was a domino effect that led to a transformation filtering into other areas of my life. These unexpected perks, awakened via my practices, allowed me to receive much more than I anticipated.

The important thing to remember is that you are unique in your personal spiritual practice. What worked for me in my journey, may not work for yours. The following may provide support when attempting to navigate yourself within your personal practices. The key is to remain open to new methods of meditation, as they will assist you in your journey and serve as a reminder that your needs will change as you continue to evolve who you are and what your needs may be. This is why I wrote earlier about meditation being a beginning of something new: you are constantly learning, evolving, and writing new chapters each and every time you sit down to meditate.

## TIME TO CONSIDER

**1) Yoga**

Introduce movement to your body by participating in various yoga practices, as there are numerous types to try. Among the several benefits yoga provides, try to see it as a chance to begin an adventure to connect to your thoughts and listen to your body's response. Yoga practice also includes meditation, as mentioned above. Yoga and meditation go hand in hand because yoga allows you to bring attention and awareness into the present moment; you have to focus your mind whilst performing challenges for your body. Yoga provides you with a moving meditative practice if you are not familiar or comfortable with seated meditation practices.

2) **Meditation**

As we know, there are many forms of practising meditation. It is easy to attempt one form of mediation and dismiss its benefits, especially if you do not give it the time, attention, or the practice it deserves. Instead, set yourself up with a few difference practices. By that I mean do one style for a few weeks and change it to another if it doesn't gel with you and how you are feeling. I encourage you to explore various methods of meditating. You may find you suit one style over another, which may then change over the course of your journey. Once you have understood which path suits you best, keep pursuing that journey until you feel an urge to change. Remember, this enables you to reconnect with your mind and body. When you begin to understand your body, you listen to your intuition, you trust the timings, and things will begin to connect.

3) **Journal**

As always, this crops up time and time again because if you can understand where you have been versus where you are now, you are more likely to be aware of where you would like to grow. This entails understanding what it is you are seeking and journaling how you feel. This is particularly useful when interpreting the effects meditation has on you. Writing your progress will provide essential analysis as you continue your individual path because it will showcase methods that work for you and which of those do not. This is particularly useful when finding out what effect meditation is having on your waking day. It is easy to miss crucial changes when you are distracted in the world; through reflection you can notice and account for these differences. Journaling an intention for your practice also serves a greater purpose and aligns you with a goal you can use within your preparation.

*When situations test you, they will allow you to reflect on how you deal with them.*
*When you grow your spiritual and emotional journey, you are no longer phased by such events; you realise it was within your power this whole time.*
*It is within your power to choose the direction you want to go during your journey.*
*It is within your power to choose the direction that fulfils your version of happiness, each and every time.*
Tulshi Varsani

When journaling, I would often reflect on my own journey. On various occasions, when encountering bad news, I would break into tears purely from the overwhelming emotions. As my meditation practices evolved, I found ways in which I was more compassionate and kinder to myself. I noticed this via waves of comfort during chaotic moments. Making choices that served my mind and wellbeing became more noticeable. It was more apparent when faced with distressing news. Previously, these circumstances would have led me into a state of emotional upset and would linger days, weeks, even months after. Now I can recognise the need to calm my breath, which brings clarity and peace of mind amongst chaos. When facing hurtful situations, I can now accept, acknowledge, and confront them as being a natural part of life. With this personal and spiritual growth, I am clearer much sooner in the way I can confront those experiences and how I can choose the direction I want to take instead. I've regained my sense of control and found clarity.

As I reflect on what I have achieved over the past few years, I understand how my journey helped me unleash the power within. All I had learnt came together to save me during a period of intense suffering. When I experienced an oncoming anxiety attack during that life-altering news at work, that was when my new habits kicked into gear. The work I had done in the dark led me to put them into practice when I needed them amongst chaotic circumstances.

# CHAPTER FIFTEEN: POSITIVE EVALUATION

*Move forward with grace and accept the unknown.*
Tulshi Varsani

Within the first two years into my spiritual journey I began noticing self-love, appreciation, compassion, and authenticity. For many years I had unknowingly, yet purposefully, blocked off affection by creating internal resistance. The love I was battling and so hopelessly seeking externally could never ignite or thrive in such a hostile environment. Since the pathway opened and revolutionised my awareness it became apparent that if I wanted the kind of love I desperately sought and craved, I needed to embody it and nurture it within myself first. I needed to start the fire and maintain it in order for it to keep me warm.

None of the countless quotes and advice on self-love ever resonated with me. The messages were foggy until I was ready to open my eyes and see the sunshine for myself. I find it is like receiving advice from a friend or relative. Though we are actively seeking advice about an issue we are facing or seek some clarity in relation to a problem, when a friend or colleague lays out the solution out in front of us, and their interpretation seems logical and fair, at the time it does not compute because so often we may be stuck in a loop and are not ready for the answers – even if it is right in front of us. Until suddenly, days (even months) later, the penny drops, and it becomes as clear as day. It is a classic interpretation of why the teacher appears when you are ready to learn. In the same way, I did not fully comprehend with the concept or practice of self-love until I was ready. Only then did the pieces fall into place: this happens only when you heighten your awareness and seek inner truth with an open heart.

Accepting and releasing control instead of forcing love into my personal life meant that I was able to focus on existing moments, rather than focusing on the lack thereof. I was able to focus on the abundance of what already existed, instead of what was missing. Shifting my focus and altering my perspective on gifts and blessings I already had allowed me to be grateful and fulfilled in the now. The need to be kinder to myself, as well as come to terms with what has been, allowed me to transfer energy towards all the things I was thankful for. Rather than pressing play on the inner critic and replaying those old, repetitive thoughts, I chose to listen to something else, rewrite the stories, and direct the momentum towards something more positive and progressive regarding my goals.

I began to shed the light on what was already around me and refocused the illumination that could shine within. This broadened my narrowed vision and opened my heart in a new direction. This pathway led me towards feeling an increased sense of appreciation and gratitude. Through this recognition and openness, I gave thanks for the relationships I already had within my life; this alone allowed for relationships to multiply. As I accepted and appreciated the loving relationships from my family and my friends, it gave me opportunities to be grateful for the love that existed all around me. Instead of looking for more or focusing on its absence, I was thankful for what I already had right now.

Incidentally, there were more of what you may class as 'coincidences' (I personally believe everything is happening for us and happens for a reason), occurring in my personal relationships; I found myself having more chance encounters within personal and professional fields; and it allowed more loving, kind, compassionate people within my life. Like a moth to a flame, I was attracting something I was already grateful for and more like-minded people were making themselves known to me. I found myself interacting with people who embraced their sympathetic, loving selves, and these interactions increased through various serendipitous events. My aim was to nurture those new relationships, friendships, and connections, allowing me to continue to be open to new personalities I could learn and grow from. Accepting the love within and around me brought plenty of pleasurable and joyful experiences. Needless to say, it also increased my overall sense of happiness.

Think about a person in your life that made you wonder why they came about. This could be your partner or closest friend. When you sit back and reflect on the friendship and/or connection you may be able to recall how much this person has supported your growth and wellbeing through various challenges or life's events. This reflection allows you to appreciate that person and those moments. This is also the case when you reflect upon relationships that did not necessarily benefit your wellbeing but gave you the ability to learn key life lessons.

Looking back at the series of relationships from your past will enable you to find where opportunities for growth lie; to awaken you and allow you to see life from a different perspective. If you are lucky to have found the person you want to be with for the rest of your life, do you ever think back to past relationships and thank God, the universe, or even your partner that they came along when they did? You may deduce the reasons the other relationships did not work was for the best. Being grateful for your past, expressing self-care for your decisions, and recognising the mistakes in your past leads to an increased state of self-acceptance. Being grateful for the journey that has brought you into a state of happiness and appreciation also allows grace in.

Being grateful and owning self-compassion – even after an unexpected event occurs – can be difficult, but these qualities *can* be cultivated. Having self-compassion gives you a newfound motivation; there is even health psychology journaled research where they found building yourself up instead of tearing yourself down can lead to better health decisions.[1] Research analysis observed 15 studies of more than 3,000 people across the age spectrum, discovering links between self-compassion and four key health-promoting behaviours such as eating better, exercising more, getting restful sleep, and stressing less. Those who were more self-compassionate practised these health habits more often. Self-compassion is often confused with self-indulgence or lowering standards. This latter behaviour may be accepted in some societies, but it is detrimental to our wellbeing. As mentioned in previous chapters, self-criticism helps motivate others but those who are low in self-compassion are harder on themselves and research reveals being kinder to yourself does not lower your standards.

*With self-compassion, you reach just as high, but if you don't reach your goals it's okay because your sense of self-worth isn't contingent on success*
Unknown[2]

Self-worth is conducive to motivation and it is healthy for you. Speaking well about yourself instead of criticising each decision can make a huge difference to your health. Once you make room for errors, and make yourself accountable for forging new pathways from that experience, you will be astounded by how much you accomplish, and continue to pursue similar achievements when you are more compassionate to yourself.

In 2007, researchers at Wake Forest University suggested that a minor self-compassion intervention influences eating habits.[2] An experiment included 84 female college students eating doughnuts. One group was given a lesson in self-compassion regarding food, before being asked to taste test sweets from large bowls. Those who were regular dieters or had guilt about forbidden foods ate far less when they heard the researchers' reassurance. However, those who were not given the message ate more. The women who felt bad about consuming the doughnuts engaged in emotional eating, whereas those who gave themselves permission enjoyed the sweets but did not overeat. The significance of this research is that it found self-compassion is key in diet and weight loss plans as many diets evolve around self-discipline, deprivation, and neglect. When I experienced emotional eating no foods brought that level of satisfaction or support I was seeking; instead, it brought a ton of shame, guilt, and sadness. Bringing awareness to the foods I ate and being conscious whilst eating meant I could enjoy all types of food and would be less likely to engage in emotional eating patterns I previously encountered.

Loving yourself also has the potential to make you feel more optimistic. Students were more likely to place self-worth on internal habits such as moral values, with studies finding they were less stressed as a result.[2] Those students tended to perform better academically, reducing the stress that can often lead to procrastination. People with increased self-compassion had fewer negative emotional reactions to both real, remembered events, and imagined, bad ones. Self-compassionate people accepted responsibility for the negative experience despite having to counteract bad feelings about it.

Another study found that a gentle, non-judgemental approach helps individuals bounce back after a major crisis.[3] Research psychologists found newly divorced people who spoke compassionately towards themselves adjusted significantly better in the ten months following their divorce compared to those who spoke more harshly to themselves. Self-compassion outperformed self-esteem and optimism as a predictor of good coping mechanisms. In chapter five you may recall I mentioned optimism doesn't need to mean denying or avoiding negative feelings. Self-compassion protects people from negative events differently; much better than self-esteem can. Positive feelings that characterise self-compassion do not appear to involve the hubristic, narcissistic, or self-enhancing illusions that characterise many people with high self-esteem. This is particularly important for those with low self-esteem who treat themselves kindly. Despite unflattering self-evaluations, they still fair better than those with high self-esteem. Self-compassionate people tend to create a view of themselves that depends less on the outcomes of events. They are also kinder as well as more accepting towards themselves whether events go well or not.

Through practising self-compassion, not only are you able to nurture your existing relationships, but you are also open to new ones. Now when you embark on the initial situation of meeting someone new, as you seek to explore this new relationship, though you do not know how it will end, you enter it with joy and excitement. The fear of its ending does not creep into your head when you first enter this new and stimulating phase. You approach it with an open heart and allow the unknown to be, because you are enjoying the present moment. Whether that relationship turns out to be positive and thrives, or eventually becomes someone you no longer have contact with, it will still teach you something you did not know before. Being kinder to yourself in all eventualities and drawing in self-compassion invites new circumstances and experiences, and can nurture your personal gratitude within those happy moments. Dr Neff, a professor of human development in Austin, Texas, accepts it is hard to unlearn habits of a lifetime, yet we should allow to actively pursue and consciously develop the habit of self-compassion.[2]

### TIME TO CONSIDER – PRACTICE MAKES PROGRESS

1) **Write a letter to yourself**
   Practise self-compassion on yourself by writing to yourself as if you are an outsider looking in. As only you know your true experiences and personal journey, no one will ever know you as well as you do, therefore take a moment and allow this to thrive.
   - Draw in aspects of what you like about yourself and what you are proud of.
   - Take a moment to appreciate yourself.
   - Appreciate your values, your morals, and your whole self.
   
   Note: it must be positive appreciation only.

2) **Journal**
   Journaling has been mentioned several times throughout this book because journaling allows you to express how you feel. By being open, compassionate, and kinder to

yourself, you will allow yourself to accept situations without judgements. This practice can cultivate self-compassion through this regular routine.

3) **Write / vlog / sing**
   - Whatever your creative expression; own it!
   - You may choose to record yourself singing, reading a poem, or vlogging.
   - What would you say to your younger self?
   - What advice would you give them?

4) **Write your own plan**
   Put aside some time to write down a mantra of kindness to yourself. This is useful when you are going through heartache or hardship. Repeat this mantra to settle your thoughts, calm your breath, and draw you back into the present moment. To begin with, it will be useful to use examples online or from the below – as long as you resonate with them. Once you become more certain of yourself and your goals you may find making up a compassionate mantra that aligns with those will be fruitful to your growth.

   You can use various statements to ground yourself, and express kindness. Here are some examples to use before creating your own.

   *I appreciate myself.*
   *I am doing the best I can.*
   *I am enough.*
   *I am patient.*
   *I am evolving.*
   *I forgive myself.*
   *I love myself.*
   *I am worthy.*
   *I am open to receiving love, from myself and others.*

5) **The power of prayer**
Whenever you are feeling less compassionate (as will happen), you may find solace in saying a small prayer to the universe or your spiritual guides:

*I acknowledge this is a moment of suffering.
I accept this moment for what it is. I know this too shall pass.*

*Whilst I am experiencing this challenge, I appreciate I am strong enough to handle this situation. I will continue to be gentle and kind to myself.*

*Please may I [insert name] grant myself the compassion I need right now.*

*As I sit here, I accept what has been and leave it behind me.
What is for me is right now and what is to come is bountiful.*

*As I am more compassionate to myself,
I am compassionate to others.*

*I exude self-compassion and it enriches all areas of my life.*

Tulshi Varsani

## CHAPTER SIXTEEN: BEGIN WITH ONE STEP

Throughout my various experiences, having assessed what happiness entails, and ways it can be cultivated, I recognise and proudly pronounce myself to exude a positive mindset, even when difficult situations arise.

What was particularly illuminating was recalling how my younger self would get agitated and irritated, even furiously angry at various situations or people, and my emotions would become overwhelming. Yet the next day I would begin afresh and start a new day with a new mindset. I lost that as I grew older and let my own fears and negativity – and sometimes other people or unexpected situations – mute that positive young girl who, though naïve, was completely happy.

Now I understand that the younger version of myself has remained within me the whole time; she never left. She is a part of who I am: a young, boisterous, compassionate, kind person who no longer needs to hide in the shadowy depths of despair. Instead, she has come out of past experiences into her truly positive, authentic, happy self. Though I understand this rollercoaster of a journey hasn't been easy, as I look back I can still appreciate what has been. Those lessons and learnings allowed me to gain courage, to strengthen my determination and resolve. They also allowed me to change habits that didn't align with growth. By nourishing the positive elements, throwing in realistic strategies, and working through the challenges I am finally able to recognise my biggest strength was overcoming things and moving forward. I choose to take the day and accept its opportunities for growth, for abundance, for learning, for advancing, for whatever it may bring.

*Through gratitude, I am grounded.*
*Through reflections, I am humbled.*
*Through fulfilment of my basic needs, I am wealthy.*
Tulshi Varsani

By realising how much I have in my life, it allows me to accept more. I understand my pursuit of happiness, what this entails, and my life's purpose. My purpose allows me to continue to strive for more, while accepting the success I already have. I understand now that happiness creates a foundation for all these things; that happiness leads to fulfilment; happiness accepts growth and opportunity in everything. This is when I accepted: happiness is its own success.

*Happiness in knowing and having faith in believing: all is well.*
Tulshi Varsani

Whatever you are going through I hope these chapters provide opportunities for you to dig deeper and cultivate your physical, mental, emotional, and spiritual health. Taking time to ask yourself difficult questions will give you the space to get to know yourself better and truly understand what it is you want and where it is you want to go – particularly in understanding what happiness and success mean to *you* and what you are willing to do for it. I am a believer that growth happens every day, should we seek it. We aren't the same person we were a year ago, neither will we be the same person months from now. In fact – I mentioned this in previous chapters – as my growth evolved and opened opportunities for more possibilities, both happiness *and* success followed. When we understand everything we have is enough, we raise awareness of what matters to us and attract more of it. We will see success and happiness revolve and expand around us. We choose who and what we are surrounded by, and we can choose again when it comes to the feelings and emotions we don't agree with.

By spreading my happiness and success via my personal encounters I hope this in turn enables you to rise up, recognise your inner worth, strive for your greatness, and unleash your potential to do more.

Try and face the following questions: be purposeful when re-evaluating your journey and be truly honest within yourself. I personally do this every year. Perhaps put a reminder in your calendar to review this in a year's time.

## FINAL EVALUATIONS

1) **Who am I?**

2) **What do I stand for?**

3) **What is important to me?**

4) **What makes me happy?**

5) **What does success look like to me?**

**Success vs happiness**
You and I will view success completely differently. Success to someone can be managing the day well, being productive in writing, focusing on a project at work, or managing to do all the things you planned with your family. For me, success was accomplishing my United Kingdom Strength and Conditioning Accreditation and I also class success as managing to pull off my mum's surprise party for her sixtieth birthday.

*Success is individual to you because it is your personal happiness.*

Tulshi Varsani

Take the following groups of people: social media moguls, actors, and musicians – they all depict models of success but know there are many ways of interpreting what defines success. However, individually each of us must put in work to define what success means to us. Go deeper into your self-worth and acknowledge what you deem to be successful. Make a list of things you identify as success. Don't be disillusioned or disheartened if the answers don't arrive straight away: use the time to digest, write it down, and walk away. It may prove useful to revisit the list a few hours or days later. You will be able to review whether your answers need adjusting. If your answers need adjusting, practise self-compassion and delve deeper into what success means to you and why that is significant. You may recognise what you wrote down pleases your family, partner, or boss. If so, see if you can find more things that make you feel successful without the need for others' approval or validation. This may be difficult at first, as there will be times when you identify or value success based on your surroundings or achieving success through interactions and material objects. Ultimately, there is no right or wrong answer for this list.

*It exists, it matters, and it is yours alone.*

Tulshi Varsani

Think about why your list would make *you* happy: does it consist of a mix in both intrinsic and extrinsic goals? Once you have assessed the things that are important to you and how they make you happy, when you have found your purpose and understood your interpretation of what success looks like, you will be more likely to align these with your goals. However, the biggest revelation will come when you realise your happiness no longer depends on outcomes (material or otherwise) and it can be manifested everywhere you go, in everything you do.

*That is your ultimate success*

# REFERENCES

**Introduction**

1 Chopra, D. (2015) '4 Steps to Turn Disappointment Into Opportunity', *Chopra Articles*, 17th April 2015. Available at: https://chopra.com/articles/4-steps-to-turn-disappointment-into-opportunity

**Chapter One**

1 Dawood, S., and Pincus, A. L. (2017) 'Pathological Narcissism and the Severity, Variability, and Instability of Depressive Symptoms. Personality Disorders: Theory, Research, and Treatment.' *Personality Disorders: Theory, Research, and Treatment*, 9(2), pp. 144–154. Advance online publication. doi: https://doi.org/10.1037/per0000239
2 Gao, X. (2016) 'Cultural differences between East Asian and North American in temporal orientation.' *Review of General Psychology*, 20(1), pp.118–127. doi: https://doi.org/10.1037/gpr0000070
3 Goldberg, S. B., Tucker, R. P., Greene, P. A., Davidson, R. J., Wampold, B. E., Kearney, D. J., & Simpson, T. L. (2018) 'Mindfulness-based Interventions for Psychiatric Disorders: A systematic review and meta-analysis.' *Clinical Psychology Review*, 59, pp.52–60. doi: https://doi.org/10.1016/j.cpr.2017.10.011
4 Nagayama, G.C. (2018) Article written by Gordon C. 'It's the Journey, Not the Destination—or Is It?', *Psychology Today*, 30th January 30, 2018. Available at: https://www.psychologytoday.com/us/blog/life-in-the-intersection/201801/its-the-journey-not-the-destination-or-is-it
5 Bernstein, G. (2019) *The Universe Has Your Back*. Available at: https://youtu.be/_vSwDvej25M
6 Futuyma, Douglas J., (2005) *Evolution*. Cumberland, MA: Sinauer.

7 Eagle, A (2010) 'Chance versus Randomness.', *Stanford Encyclopedia of Philosophy*. Published 18th August 2010; substantive revision 8th February 2018. Available at: https://plato.stanford.edu/entries/chance-randomness/

**Chapter Two**

1 Nahin RL, *et al.* (2016) 'Evidence-based Evaluation of Complementary Health Approaches for Pain Management in the United States.' *Mayo Clin Proceedings*, pp.1292–1306. doi: https://doi.org/10.1016/j.mayocp.2016.06.007.
2 Seppala, E. (2012) 'How the Stress of Disaster Brings People Together', *Scientific American*, 6th November 2012. Available at: https://www.scientificamerican.com/article/how-the-stress-of-disaster-brings-people-together/
3 Seligman, M. (2017) *Authentic Happiness*. London: Nicholas Brealey Publishing.

**Chapter Three**

1 Hallowell, E. H. (1997) 'Fighting Life's "What Ifs"' *Psychology Today*, 1st November 1997. Available at: https://www.psychologytoday.com/us/articles/199711/fighting-lifes-what-ifs

**Chapter Four**

1 Wrzesniewski, A., McCauley, C., Rozin, P., & Schwartz, B. (1997) 'Jobs, Careers, and Callings: People Relations to Their Work.' *Journal of Research in Personality*, pp.21–33.
2 Nettel, D. (no date) 'Types of Happiness in Psychology', *The World Counts*. Available at: https://www.theworldcounts.com/happiness/types-of-happiness-in-psychology
3 Achor, S. (no date) *The Happy Secret to Better Work.* Available at: https://www.ted.com/talks/shawn_achor_the_happy_secret_to_better_work (Accessed: 29 March 2023)

4 Klein, A. (2019) 'Working for Happiness: 7 Principles of Positive Psychology', *BrainWorld*, 8th February 2019. Available at: https://brainworldmagazine.com/working-for-happiness-7-principles-of-positive-psychology/
5 Lebowitz, S., and Akhtar, A. (2019) '14 Rich and Powerful People Share Their Surprising Definitions of Success', *Business Insider*, 29th May 2019. Available at: https://www.businessinsider.com/how-successful-people-define-success-2017-3?r=US&IR=T
6 Martinez, G. (2018) 'Everything You Know About the Fate of Lottery Winners is Probably Wrong, According to Science, *TIME*, 18th October 2018. Available at: https://time.com/5427275/lottery-winning-happiness-debunked/
7 Schmitz, T.W., Rosa, E.D. and Anderson, A.K. (2009) 'Opposing Influences of Affective State Valence on Visual Cortical Encoding.' *The Journal of Neuroscience*. 3 June 2009, 29 (22) pp.7199–7207.
8 Maack, M. M. (2017) 'Scandinavian Work Culture is Better Than Yours – Here's Why, *The Next Web*, 20th February 2017. Available at: https://thenextweb.com/business/2017/02/20/scandinavian-work-culture-is-better-than-yours/

**Chapter Five**

1 Scott, S. (2023) 'How Optimism Affects Your Happiness', *Happier Human*, 8th February 2023. Available at: https://www.happierhuman.com/optimism-happiness
2 Carver, C. S., Scheier, M. F., and Segerstrom, S. C. (2010) 'Optimism', *Clinical Psychology Review*, pp. 879–889.
3 Chemers, M. M., Watson, C. B., and May, S. T. (2000) 'Dispositional Affect and Leadership Effectiveness: A Comparison of Self-esteem, Optimism, and Efficacy', *Personality and Social Psychology Bullletin*, pp. 267–277.
4 Dholakia, U. (2016). '4 Ways In Which Optimism Helps Entrepreneurs Succeed', *Psychology Today*, 2nd October 2016. Available at: https://www.psychologytoday.com/us/blog/the-science-

behind-behavior/201610/4-ways-in-which-optimism-helps-entrepreneurs-succeed
5 Aidis, R., Mickiewicz, T., & Sauka, A. (2008) *DeepBlue*. Retrieved from Why Are Optimistic Entrepreneurs Successful?: https://www.psychologytoday.com/us/blog/the-science-behind-behavior/201610/4-ways-in-which-optimism-helps-entrepreneurs-succeed
6 Seligman, M. (2017) *Authentic Happiness*. London: Nicholas Brealey Publishing.
7 Health, H. T. (2012) 'Positive Feelings May Help Protect Cardiovascular Health', *Psychological Bulletin*. Available from: https://www.eurekalert.org/pub_releases/2012-04/hsop-pfm041312.php
8 Tindle, H. A., *et al.* (2009) 'Optimism, Cynical Hostility, and Incident Coronary Heart Disease and Mortality in the Women's Health Initiative', *Circulation*, pp. 656–662.
9 Scott, S. (2023) 'How Optimism Affects Your Happiness', *Happier Human*, 8th February 2023. Available at: https://www.happierhuman.com/optimism-happiness

**Chapter Six**

1 Barr, S. (2019) 'Six Ways Social Media Negatively Affects Your Mental Health', *The Independent*, 19th January 2022. Available at: https://www.independent.co.uk/life-style/health-and-families/social-media-mental-health-negative-effects-depression-anxiety-addiction-memory-a8307196.html
2 Krumhuber, E. *et al.* (2007) 'Facial Dynamics as Indicators of Trustworthiness and Cooperative Behaviour' *Emotion*, pp.730–735.
3 Widrich, L. (2013) 'The Science of Smiling: A Guide to the World's Most Powerful Gesture', *Buffer*, 9th April 2013. Available at: https://buffer.com/resources/the-science-of-smiling-a-guide-to-humans-most-powerful-gesture/
4 *The Scotsman* (2005) 'One Smile Can Make You Feel Like a Million Dollars'. Updated 4th March 2005. Available at: https://www.scotsman.com/health/one-smile-can-make-you-feel-million-dollars-2469850

5 Buck, R. (1980) 'The Facial Feedback Hypothesis', *Journal of Personality and Social Psychology*, pp.811–824.
6 Stepper, S., and Strack, F. (1993) 'Proprioceptive Determinants of Emotional and Nonemotional Feelings', *Journal of Personality and Social Psychology*, pp.211–220.
7 Abel, E. L., and Kruger, M. L. (2010) 'Smile Intensity in Photographs Predicts Longevity', *Psychology Science*, pp. 542–544.
8 Ranganathan, V. K., Siemionow, V., Liu, J. Z., Sahgal, V., and Yue, G. H. (2004) 'From Mental Power to Muscle Power', *Neuropsychologia*, pp.944–956.

**Chapter Seven**

1 Townley, C. (2018) 'How do relationship breakups impact physical activity?', *Medical News Today*, 26th December 2018. Available at: https://www.medicalnewstoday.com/articles/323987.php#2
2 'Obesity and Overweight', *World Health Organisation*, 9th June 2021. Available at: https://www.who.int/news-room/fact-sheets/detail/obesity-and-overweight
3 'What is BDNF and What Does it Do?' (2016) *Examined Existence*, 29th April 2016. Available at: https://examinedexistence.com/what-is-bdnf-and-what-does-it-do/
4 Cotman, C. W. (no date) 'Exercise induces BDNF, improves learning and reduces B-amyloid' Available at: https://examinedexistence.com/what-is-bdnf-and-what-does-it-do/
5 *The Significance of BDNF for Learning, Memory, and Cognitive Function* (2018) Available at: https://therevisionist.org/reviews/the-significance-of-bdnf-for-learning-memory-and-cognitive-function/
6 Coulson, J., McKenna, J., and Field, M. (2008) 'Exercising at Work and Self-reported Work Performance', *International Journal of Workplace Health Management*, pp. 176–197.
7 Pronk, N. P., Martinson, B., Kessler, R. C., Beck, A. L., Simon, G. E., and Wang, P. (2004) 'The Association Between Work Performance and Physical Activity, Cardiorespiratory

Fitness, and Obesity', *The Journal of Occupational and Environmental Medicine*, pp.19–25.
8 Pozen, R. C. (2012) *'Exercise Increases Productivity'*, *Brookings*, 24th October 2012. Available at: https://www.brookings.edu/opinions/exercise-increases-productivity/
9 Berman, M. G., Jonides, J., and Kaplan, S. (2008) 'The Cognitive Benefits of Interacting With Nature', *Psychological Science*, pp.1207–12.
10 *How to Increase Your Productivity by 21% with Exercise* (no date). Available at: https://productivityist.com/increase-productivity-21-exercise/
11 Ballard, J. (2019) 'Millennials Are the Loneliest Generation', *YouGov*, 30th July 2019. Available at: https://today.yougov.com/topics/lifestyle/articles-reports/2019/07/30/loneliness-friendship-new-friends-poll-survey
12 Chang PJ, W. L. (2014) 'Social Relationships, Leisure Activity, and Health in Older Adults', *Health Psychology*, 33(6) pp.516–523.
13 Cohen, S. (2004) 'Social Relationships and Health', American Psychologist, pp. 676–684.
14 Morgan, G. W.S. (2019) 'A Life Fulfilled: Positively Influencing Physical Activity in Older Adults – a Systematic Review and Meta-ethnography', *BMC Public Health* 19(1), 362.
15 Mokeyane, K.N. (2017) 'Does Physical Development Influence Children's Emotional Development?', *How to (Adult)*, 26th September. Available at: https://howtoadult.com/physical-development-influence-childrens-emotional-development-19539.html
16 Rick Nauert, P. (2019) 'Physical Activity Helps Improve Social Skills', *PsychCentral*, 15th June 2019. Available at: https://psychcentral.com/news/2018/03/15/physical-activity-helps-improve-social-skills/12120.html
17 Diener E and Seligman ME (2002) 'Very Happy People', *Psychol Sci.* 2002 Jan;13(1) pp. 81–4. doi: https://doi.org/10.1111/1467-9280.00415

18 Theresa E. DiDonato, P. (2014) '5 Reasons Why Couples Who Sweat Together, Stay Together', *Psychology Today*, 10th January 2014. Available at: https://www.psychologytoday.com/gb/blog/meet-catch-and-keep/201401/5-reasons-why-couples-who-sweat-together-stay-together

19 Hibbert, D. C. (no date) *8 Keys to Mental Health Through Exercise*. Available at: http://www.drchristinahibbert.com/wp-content/uploads/2012/03/8-Keys-to-Mental-Health-Through-Exercise-1.pdf

**Chapter Eight**

1 *Definition & Facts for Binge Eating Disorder* (last reviewed May 2021), National Institute of Diabetes and Digestive and Kidney Diseases (NIH). Available at: https://www.niddk.nih.gov/health-information/weight-management/binge-eating-disorder/definition-facts#common

2 Michigan State University (2013) 'The Biology behind Binge Eating', 1st May 2013. Available at: https://www.sciencedaily.com/releases/2013/05/130501101304.htm

3 Wansink B, P. J. (2005) 'Bottomless Bowls: Why Visual Cues of Portion Size May Influence Intake. *Obesity Research & Clinical Practice*, pp. 93–100.

4 Warren JM, S. N. (2017) 'A Structured Literature Review on the Role of Mindfulness, Mindful Eating and Intuitive Eating in Changing Eating Behaviours: Effectiveness and Associated Potential Mechanisms', *Nutrition Research Reviews*, pp.272–283.

5 U.S. Department of Health and Human Services and U.S. Department of Agriculture *2015 – 2020 dietary guidelines*, 8th edition. Available at: https://health.gov/our-work/food-nutrition/2015-2020-dietary-guidelines/guidelines/chapter-1/the-science-behind-healthy-eating-patterns/

6 Public Health England Nutition Advice Team (2018) *A Quick Guide to the Government's Healthy Eating Recommendations*. Available at: https://assets.publishing.service.gov.uk/government/uploads/

system/uploads/attachment_data/file/742746/A_quick_guide_to_govt_healthy_eating_update.pdf
7 Diet and Mental Health article by Mental Health Foundation. (Last updated version 25th January 2022) Available at: Diet and mental health | Mental Health Foundation
8 Saunders, S., and Streets, A. (2019) 'Happy Ever After: 25 Ways to Live Well into Old Age', *The Guardian*, 29th May 2019. Available at: https://www.theguardian.com/lifeandstyle/2019/may/26/happy-ever-after-25-ways-to-live-well-into-old-age
9 Dipnall JF, P. J. (2017) 'Getting RID of the Blues: Formulating a Risk Index for Depression (RID) Using Structural Equation Modeling', *Australian & New Zealand Journal of Psychiatry*, pp. 1121–1133.
10 Lakkur S, J. S. (2015) 'Diet and Stroke: Recent Evidence Supporting a Mediterranean-Style Diet and Food in the Primary Prevention of Stroke', *Stroke*, pp. 2007–2011.
11 Madhuleena Roy Chowdhury, B. (2020) 'The Neuroscience of Gratitude and How It Affects Anxiety & Grief', *Positive Psychology*, 1st September 2020. Available at: https://positivepsychology.com/neuroscience-of-gratitude/
12 Mountjoy, M., Sundot-Borgen, J., Burke, L., Ackerman, K. E., Blauwet, C., Constantini, N., & Lundy, B. (2018) 'International Olympic Committee (IOC) consensus statement on relative energy deficiency in sport (RED-S)': 2018 update. *International Journal of Sport Nutrition and Exercise Metabolism*, 28(4), 316-331.

**Chapter Nine**

1 National Heart, Lung, and Blood institute (last updated 24th March 2022) 'What are sleep deprivation and deficiency?' Available at: Sleep Deprivation and Deficiency - What Are Sleep Deprivation and Deficiency? | NHLBI, NIH
2 Taylor, Ian (2022), *BBC Science Focus Magazine*.
3 Summer, J & Singh, A. (2023) 'What is REM sleep and how much do you need?' Available at: REM Sleep: What It Is and Why It Matters | Sleep Foundation

4 Kitamura, S. K. *et al.* (2016) 'Estimating Individual Optimal Sleep Duration and Potential Sleep Debt', *International Journal of Scientific Reports*, 6, 35812. Doi: https://doi.org/10.1038/srep35812

5 Kalb, C (2013) 'Your Alarm Clock May Be Hazardous to Your Health', *Smithsonian Magazine*, January 2013. Available at: https://www.smithsonianmag.com/science-nature/your-alarm-clock-may-be-hazardous-to-your-health-164620290/

6 Christensen MA, B. L. *et al.* (2016) 'Direct Measurements of Smartphone ScreenTime: Relationships with Demographics and Sleep' *Plos One* 9;11 (11). Doi: https://doi.org/10.1371/journal.pone.0165331

7 Michigan State University (2014) *'Nighttime Smartphone Use Zaps Workers' energy'*, 22nd January 2014. Available at: https://msutoday.msu.edu/news/2014/nighttime-smartphone-use-zaps-workers-energy/

8 YouGov (2022), *YouGov Results – Sleep Study*, (fieldwork dates 1st–5th February 2022. Available at: Big Surveys Sleep Study (w) (2).xlsx (yougov.com)

9 Walker, M. (2017) *Why We Sleep*. London: Penguin Books Ltd.

10 Newsom, R (2020) (medically reviewed by Dr Anis Rehman) 'Diet, Exercise and Sleep', *Sleep Foundation*, updated 3rd March 2023. Available at: https://www.sleepfoundation.org/articles/diet-exercise-and-sleep

11 British Lung Foundation (no date) 'OSA UK health economics report'. Available at: Month Year (blf.org.uk)

12 Kline, C. (2014) 'The Bidirectional Relationship Between Exercise and Sleep: Implications for Exercise Adherence and Sleep Improvement'. *Am J Lifestyle Med*, pp.375–379.

13 Reid KJ, B. K. (2010) 'Aerobic exercise improves self-reported sleep and quality of life in older adults with insomnia', *Journal of Clinical Sleep Medicine*, pp. 934–940.

14 Dolezal, B., Neufeld, E. V., Boland, D. M., Martin, J. L., and Cooper, C. B. (2017) 'Interrelationship between Sleep and Exercise: A Systematic Review', *Advances in Preventative Medicine*, vol. 2017. Doi: https://doi.org/10.1155/2017/1364387

15 ReShel, A. (2016) 'The Science Behind Yoga', *Awaken*, 4th June 2016. Available at: https://awaken.com/2016/06/the-science-behind-yoga/
16 Eagleson, C., Hayes, S., Mathews, A., Perman, G. and Hirsch, C. R. (2016) 'The Power of Positive Thinking: Pathological Worry is Reduced By Thought Replacement in Generalized Anxiety Disorder', *Behaviour Research and Therapy*, 78, pp. 13–18.
17 Cleveland Clinic (Health Essentials article) (2020) 'Why You Should Limit Alcohol Before Bed for Better Sleep', 17th June 2020. Available at: https://health.clevelandclinic.org/why-you-should-limit-alcohol-before-bed-for-better-sleep/ (Accessed 15th November 2022).
18 Haak, E. (2016) 'The Mistake Most People Make After Getting Too Little Sleep', *Oprah.com*, 13th July 2016. Available at: https://www.oprah.com/health_wellness/dont-go-to-bed-early-after-bad-nights-sleep

**Chapter Ten**

1 Zahn R, M. J. (2009) 'The Neural Basis of Human Social Values: Evidence from Functional MRI', *Cereb Cortex*, 19 (2), pp. 276–283.
2 Emmons, R. A. (2003) 'Counting Blessings Versus Burdens: an Experimental Investigation of Gratitude and Subjective Well-being in Daily Life', *Journal of Personality and Social Psychology*, 84, pp. 377–389.
3 Mindvalley Academy (no date) 'The Health Benefits of Gratitude: 6 Scientifically Proven Ways Being Grateful Rewires Your Brain + Body for Health'. Available at: https://www.consciouslifestylemag.com/benefits-of-gratitude-research/
4 Kobayashi A, Y. S. (2020) 'Increased Grey Matter Volume of the Right Superior Temporal Gyrus in Healthy Children with Autistic Cognitive Style: A VBM Study.' *Brain Cogn.*, 139:105514.
5 Alex Korb, P. (2012) 'The Grateful Brain', *Psychology Today*, 20th November 2012. Available at:

https://www.psychologytoday.com/us/blog/prefrontal-nudity/201211/the-grateful-brain
6 Khasdan, T. B., Uswatte, G., and Julian, T. (2006) 'Gratitude and Hedonic and Eudaimonic Well-being in Vietnam War Veterans', *Behaviour Research and Therapy*, 44 (2), pp. 177–199.
7 Fredrickson, B. L. (2003) 'What Good Are Positive Emotions in Crisis? A Prospective Study of Resilience and Emotions Following the Terrorist Attacks on the United States on September 11th, 2001', *Journal of Personality and Social Psychology*, 84 (2), pp. 365–376.
8 Emmons, R. A. and McCullough, M. E. (2003) 'Counting Blessings versus Burdens: An Experimental Investigation of Gratitude and Subjective Well-being in Daily Life.' *Journal of Personality and Social psychology*, 84, pp. 377–389.
9 Digdon, N., and Koble, A. (2011) 'Effects of Constructive Worry, Imagery Distraction, and Gratitude Interventions on Sleep Quality: A Pilot Trial', *International Association of Applied Psychology*. Doi: https://doi.org/10.1111/j.1758-0854.2011.01049.x
10 Di Fabio Annamaria, P. L., Palazzeschi, L and Bucci, O (2017) 'Gratitude in Organizations: A Contribution for Healthy Organizational Contexts', *Frontiers in Psychology*, 8, 2025.
11 Algoe, S. B. (2012) 'Find, Remind, and Bind: The Functions of Gratitude in Everyday Relationships' *Compass*, 6 (6), pp. 455–469. Doi: https://doi.org/10.1111/j.1751-9004.2012.00439.x
12 Grant AM, and Gino, G. F. (2010) 'A Little Thanks Goes a Long Way: Explaining Why Gratitude Expressions Motivate Prosocial Behavior', *Personality and Social Psychology Review*, 98 (6), pp. 946–955.
13 Seligman, M. (2017) *Authentic Happiness*. London: Nicholas Brealey Publishing.

## Chapter Eleven

1 Marks, M. L., Mirvis, P., and Ashkena, R. (2014) 'Rebounding from Career Setbacks', *Harvard Business Review*, October 2014. Available at: https://hbr.org/2014/10/rebounding-from-career-setbacks
2 Psycom editors (2016) 'The Five Stages of Grief', *Pysco*, updated 7th June 2022. Available at: https://www.psycom.net/depression.central.grief.html
3 DeCastro R, S. D. (2013) 'Batting 300 is Good: Perspectives of Faculty Researchers and Their Mentors on Rejection, Resilience, and Persistence in Academic Medical Careers', *Academic Medicine*, 88 (4), pp. 497–504.
4 Noble, J. (2020) 'Vettel "surprised" by Ferrari exit decision, no deal offered', *Motorsport.com*, 2nd July 2020. Available at: https://www.motorsport.com/f1/news/vettel-surprised-ferrari-call-binotto/4821771/
5 Wladawsky-Berger, I. (2020) 'The Long-Term Impact of Early-Career Setbacks, *Irving Wladawsky-Berger*, 25th July 2020. Available at: https://blog.irvingwb.com/blog/2020/07/the-long-term-impact-of-early-career-setbacks.html

## Chapter Twelve

1 Berman MG, J. J. (2006) 'Studying Mind and Brain with fMRI', *Social Cognitive and Affective Neuroscience*, 1 (2), pp. 158–161.
2 Varsani, T. (2020, June 14th) *Tulshi Varsani – Coach*, 14th June. Available at: https://www.youtube.com/channel/UCuuFRiSE0RZbv6bzTibg_Og
3 Herrera, T. (2019) 'How Early-Career Setbacks Can Set You Up for Success', *The New York Times*, 29th October 2019. Available at: https://www.nytimes.com/2019/10/27/smarter-living/career-advice-overcome-setback.html
4 Loscalzo, J. (2014) 'A Celebration of Failure', *Circulation*, 129 (9), pp. 953–955.

5 Powers CA, M. C. (2005) 'Predictive Modeling of Total Healthcare Costs Using Pharmacy Claims Data: a Comparison of Alternative Econometric Cost Modeling Techniques', *Medical Care*, 43 (11), pp. 1065–72.
6 Northwestern University (2019) 'Failure Prognosis: Data Science Predicts Which Failures Will Ultimately Succeed', *Science Daily*, 30th October 2019. Available at: https://www.sciencedaily.com/releases/2019/10/191030151436.htm

**Chapter Thirteen**

1 MacKenzie, S. (2020) 'How the World Happiness Report is Measuring Our Wellbeing', *The Big Issue*, 24th January 2020. Available at: https://www.bigissue.com/latest/how-the-world-happiness-report-is-measuring-our-wellbeing/
2 Twenge, J. M. (2019) 'The Sad State of Happiness in the United States and the Role of Digital Media', *World Happiness Report*, 20th March 2019. Available at: https://worldhappiness.report/ed/2019/the-sad-state-of-happiness-in-the-united-states-and-the-role-of-digital-media/
3 Wheelwright, T. (2022) 'Cell Phone Usage Statistics: How Obsessed Are We?', *Reviews.org*, 24th January. Available at: https://www.reviews.org/mobile/cell-phone-addiction/
4 Barr, S. (2019) 'Six ways social media negatively affects your mental health', *The Independent*, 10th October. Available at: https://www.independent.co.uk/life-style/health-and-families/social-media-mental-health-anxiety-b1996486.html
5 Association for Psychological Science (2017) 'Teens Unlikely to be Harmed by Moderate Screen Use', 13th January. https://www.eurekalert.org/pub_releases/2017-01/afps-tut011217.php

**Chapter Fourteen**

1 Mead, E. (2019) 'The History and Origin of Meditation', *PositivePsychology.com*, 27th May. Available at: https://positivepsychology.com/history-of-meditation/

2 Benson, H. (1983) 'The Relaxation Response: Its Subjective and Objective Historical Precedents and Physiology', *Trends in Neuroscience*, 6, pp. 281–284.
3 Kabat-Zinn, J. (no date) 'About Jon Kabat-Zinn', *jonkabatzinn.com*. Available at: https://www.mindfulnesscds.com/pages/about-the-author
4 Swami Rama Society (no date) *Swami Rama*. Available at: https://www.swamiramasociety.org/swami-rama/
5 Jain, F. A., Walsh, R. N., Eisendrath, S. J., Christensen, S., and Cahn, R. B. (2014) 'Critical Analysis of the Efficacy of Meditation Therapies for Acute and Subacute Phase Treatment of Depressive Disorders: A Systematic Review', *Psychosomatics* 56 (2), pp. 140–152.
6 Morgane, P. J., Galler, J. R., and Mokler, D. J. (2005) 'A Review of Systems and Networks of the Limbic Forebrain/limbic Midbrain', *Progress in Neurobiology*, 75, pp. 143–160.
7 James W. Anderson, C. L. (2008) 'Blood Pressure Response to Transcendental Meditation: A Meta-analysis', *American Journal of Hypertension*, 21 (3), pp. 310–316.
8 Rainforth, M. S. (2007) 'Stress Reduction Programs in Patients with Elevated Blood Pressure: A Systematic Review and Meta-analysis', *Current Science Inc*, 9 (6), pp. 520–528.
9 Tomljenović, H., and Begić, D. (2016) 'Changes in trait brainwave power and coherence, state and trait anxiety after three-month transcendental meditation (TM) practice', *Psychiatria Danubina*, 28, pp. 63–72. Available at: https://www.researchgate.net/publication/301778817_Chang es_in_trait_brainwave_power_and_coherence_state_and_tr ait_anxiety_after_three-
month_transcendental_meditation_TM_practice
10 Gaylord, S., Palsson, O., Garland, E., Faurot, K., Coble, R., Mann, D. and Whitehead, W. (2011) 'Mindfulness Training Reduces the Severity of Irritable Bowel Syndrome in Women: Results of a Randomized Controlled Trial.' *American Journal of Gastroenterology*, 106 (9), pp. 1678–1688.
11 Norris C. J., Creem D., Hendler R., and Kober H. (2018) 'Brief Mindfulness Meditation Improves Attention in Novices: Evidence From ERPs and Moderation by Neuroticism',

*Frontiers in Human Neuroscience*, 12, p. 315. Available at: https://www.frontiersin.org/articles/10.3389/fnhum.2018.00315
12 Lagrosen, Y., and Travis, F. T. (2015) 'Exploring the Connection Between Quality Management and Brain Functioning', *The TQM Journal*, 27 (5), pp. 565–575.
13 Rubik, B. (2011) 'Neurofeedback-Enhanced Gamma Brainwaves from the Prefrontal Cortical Region of Meditators and Non-Meditators and Associated Subjective Experiences', *Journal of alternative and complementary medicine*, 17 (2), pp. 109–115.
14 Nidich, S., Mjasiri, S., Nidich, R., Rainforth, M., Grant, J., Valosek, L., and Zigler, R. (2011) 'Academic Achievement and Transcendental Meditation: A Study with At-Risk Urban Middle School Students', *Education*, 131 (3), pp. 556–564. Available at: https://eric.ed.gov/?id=EJ996375
15 Jha, A. P., Krompinger, J., Baime, M.J., (2007) 'Mindfulness Training Modifies Subsystems of Attention', *Cognitive Affective & Behavioral Neuroscience*, 7, pp. 109–119.
16 Aron, E., & Aron, A. (1982) 'Transcendental Meditation Program and Marital Adjustment' *Psychological Reports*, 51 (3), pp. 887–890.
17 Carson, J. W., Carson, K. M., Gil, K. M., & Bauocm, D. H. (2004) 'Mindfulness-based Relationship Enhancement', *Behavior Therapy*, 35 (3), pp. 471–494.

**Chapter Fifteen**

1 Oaklander, M. (2014) 'The Reason You Make Unhealthy Choices', *Time*, 25th September. Available at: https://time.com/3430670/self-compassion-health/
2 Parker-Pope, T. (2011) 'Go Easy on Yourself, a New Wave of Research Urges', *The New York Times*, 28th February. Available at: https://well.blogs.nytimes.com/2011/02/28/go-easy-on-yourself-a-new-wave-of-research-urges/

3 Krakovsky, M. (2012) 'Self-Compassion Fosters Mental Health', *Scientific American Mind*, 1st July. Available at: https://www.scientificamerican.com/article/self-compassion-fosters-mental-health/

## ACKNOWLEDGEMENTS

Thank you to all my friends and family who supported me on my journey while writing this book! Thank you, Mukesh Varsani: you are an inspiration and as a child I loved everything you loved and I am so happy we get to share this incredible friendship as adults. Your words of advice are the ones I value! Thanks to Kelly Beahan-Smith, my friend, confidante, and podcast co-host, you mean so much to me. You allow me to tap into my own intuition and always provide a loving, kind ear to listen when I need some wisdom!

Thank you to Esther Dickinson for all our conversations about writing, books, and creative ventures! Cannot wait to share more of these writing adventures with you! Thank you to Nitesh Patel, your unwavering support and thought-provoking conversations have been incredibly valuable. Thank you to Allie Van Fossen who supported my recovery post-burnout via your online yin yoga classes. You continue to be an inspiration to my YouTube channel and online presence.

To my editor, Siân Smith, your enthusiasm for working with female authors in the health and wellness space made me feel in safe hands, making the editing process so easy and enjoyable. The dread ended up a beautiful experience with your support! Thank you to Becky and Raven Crest Books for the formatting when hitting a wall with self-publishing.

Thanks to Geoff Willis; one of a few people who read the book in its earliest stages and who encouraged me to step forward with the editing. To Louise Collings, I appreciate all the support during the trying moments of my work in high performance and being a friend when you were also going through tough times, which meant we could lean on one another! Thank you for hearing me, offering your support and reading this manuscript in its first stages of life! Thank you, Jess Cooke, for the inspiration when you asked me about how

you wanted to bottle up my enthusiastic nature!
Thanks also to the following individuals: Richard Husseiny, Julie Gooderick, Bridgitte Swales, Sophia Nimphius, James Baker, Mike Young, Monica Simmons, Steph Tranter, Sue Anstiss MBE, Catherine King, Rich Wharton, Ian Jeffries, Lee Eldridge, James Hewitt, Gerry Convy, Dr Ford Dyke, Pete McKnight, John Fernandes, Simon Brundish, James Vowles, Toto Wolff, and Robert Yeowart for all believing in me, supporting my coaching career through its stages, and the knowledge, advice and the many laughs we've shared.

Thank you to my parents for everything they do and all my many friends and family who own who they are and allow me to be unapologetically me, I love you for it! Thank you and much love to my nieces and nephews who constantly remind me how to incorporate joy, enthusiasm, and play when I'm around them!

Printed in Great Britain
by Amazon